ASTD Training Basics Series

D1232581

EVALUATION
Basics

DONALD V. McCAIN

A Complete, How-to
Guide to Help You:

- Use Evaluation to Drive Performance

- Develop a Comprehensive
  Evaluation Plan

- Demonstrate Value
  and Communicate Results

⚘ ASTD Press

ASTD Press is an internationally renowned source of insightful and practical information on workplace learning and performance topics, including training basics, evaluation and return-on-investment (ROI), instructional systems development (ISD), e-learning, leadership, and career development.

Ordering information: Books published by ASTD Press can be purchased by visiting our Website at store.astd.org or by calling 800.628.2783 or 703.683.8100.

Library of Congress Control Number: 2004116269

ISBN-10: 1-56286-373-8
ISBN-13: 978-1-56286-373-9

Acquisitions and Development Editor: Mark Morrow
Copyeditor: Karen Eddleman
Interior Design and Production: Kathleen Schaner
Cover Design: Ana Ilieva
Cover Illustration: Phil and Jim Bliss

Table of Contents

About the
Training Basics Series

A STD's *Training Basics* series recognizes and, in some ways, celebrates the fast-paced, ever-changing reality of organizations today. Jobs, roles, and expectations change quickly. One day you might be a network administrator or a process line manager, and the next day you might be asked to train 50 employees in basic computer skills or to instruct line workers in quality processes.

Where do you turn for help? The ASTD *Training Basics* series is designed to be your one-stop solution. The series takes a minimalist approach to your learning curve dilemma and presents only the information you need to be successful. Each book in the series guides you through key aspects of training: giving presentations, making the transition to the role of trainer, designing and delivering training, and evaluating training. The books in the series also include some advanced skills such as performance and basic business proficiencies.

The ASTD *Training Basics* series is the perfect tool for training and performance professionals looking for easy-to-understand materials that will prepare non-trainers to take on a training role. In addition, this series is the perfect reference tool for any trainer's bookshelf and a quick way to hone your existing skills. The titles currently planned for the series include:

- ▶ *Presentation Basics* (2003)
- ▶ *Trainer Basics* (2003)
- ▶ *Training Design Basics* (2003)
- ▶ *Facilitation Basics* (2004)
- ▶ *Communication Basics* (2004)
- ▶ *Performance Basics* (2004)
- ▶ *Evaluation Basics* (2005)
- ▶ *Needs Assessment Basics* (2005)
- ▶ *ROI Basics* (2005)
- ▶ *Organizational Development Basics* (2005).

Preface

O rganizations invest millions of dollars in training programs, some purchased and some internally developed. Although we *hope* they are effective, our internal clients *demand* that they are effective. The question is: What does effective mean? Is it that the participants had a good time? Much of what we do involves an element of entertainment. A potential client was explaining a change management training program he was providing for hourly workers. The participants loved it because the facilitator made them laugh. They had a good time. So, is this a measure of effectiveness? Even though the course participants may say yes, your client may very well say no. Effectiveness for clients means learning, application, and impact—not just the learners' reactions.

Another story may make the point. A client wanted an account management course for her sales professionals. During a design meeting, the client came in and almost shouted, "I want to know how we know if the salespeople are learning anything and if they are using it!" It was good that these aspects of evaluation were built into the course. As it turns out, the learning director had just come from a meeting with a vice president of sales who indicated that he was withdrawing all support until the training organization could demonstrate that the training was making a difference. For example, were the salespeople learning anything? And, if they were learning, were they using the content?

These examples illustrate that training effectiveness includes learning, use on the job, and impact. Indeed, an evaluation plan should provide for each of these elements and implement them to the extent that the client wants to see results. This means that the client determines the extent of the evaluation effort.

Who Can Benefit From This Book?

This book is written for people who want to enhance their skills in evaluating learning experiences in an organizational environment. That group might include designers or developers of training; training or human resource professionals or managers who contract with vendor companies and want to evaluate their course offerings; subject matter experts who occasionally function in a training role or who are moving into a training role in their jobs; facilitators who want to enhance their evaluation skills; and trainers whose organizations are holding the training function accountable for both learners' performance on the job and organizational impact.

The purpose of this book is to facilitate your learning and enhance your evaluation skills. As you enhance your skills, you will provide higher-quality course design, offer better learning experiences for your participants, deliver specific feedback tailored to particular audiences, and make a real and positive contribution to your organization.

Acknowledgments

I want to give a special thanks to Deborah Tobey of Deb Tobey LLC who provided invaluable insights and assistance into the writing of this book. She is a trusted friend and a true professional who uses her expertise to further the profession.

I would like to dedicate this book to my spouse, Kathy McCain, who provided support throughout this endeavor.

Don McCain
February 2005

Introduction: Evaluation for You and for Your Client

 What's Inside This Chapter

In this chapter, you'll learn:

▶ How *Evaluation Basics* can support and enhance your skills as an evaluator or designer
▶ How to locate information in the book using a chapter-by-chapter outline
▶ How to use the icons as guides to special material in the book.

How *Evaluation Basics* Can Help You

Evaluation can be beneficial to you as a course designer or evaluator. Information gleaned from evaluation can be used to improve your courseware, improve facilitation skills, and position your learning experiences as value added. Furthermore, evaluation can help build relationships with your internal and external clients, and gain support from your internal clients.

The evaluation challenge is one of balance. You must do enough analysis to meet your own needs while also meeting the needs of your client. Too much evaluation is a waste of effort; not enough analysis inhibits good decision making. This is why evaluation planning is so important. As part of the design process, you determine

Noted

Learning experiences are planned experiences for which the acquisition of new knowledge, skills, and abilities are the intended outcomes.

the initial business metric (the data you will track, for example, number of sales, number of defects, or turnover rates), what evaluation level of information to gather, when to gather that information, and how it will be used.

Evaluation is about quality and about making learning better. The process starts at the beginning of the design process and continues long after the learners return to their jobs. Evaluation is a process, supported by methods, tools, and instruments. It is not something you just do at the end of a course. It is something you do before, during, and after the course.

Basic Rule 1
Evaluation is a process, not an event.

Chapter-by-Chapter Highlights

Your success as an evaluator depends on your ability to gather information, analyze that information, and make and implement recommendations based on your findings. You must identify what you want to know and how you will use the information; that is, you need to identify beforehand what decision you need to make. Each chapter in *Evaluation Basics* focuses on a critical aspect of developing and implementing an evaluation plan. Here's a summary of the nine chapters in *Evaluation Basics:*

1. "Introduction: Evaluation for You and for Your Client." Right now you are engaged in an overview of the book, establishing the premise that evaluation is a process that starts with the learning design and continues all the way to assessing organizational impact. Also described in this chapter are the icons used in the book and how the icons can help you get the most out of the information presented.

2. "An Overview of Evaluation." This chapter presents an understanding of evaluation, the purposes and benefits of evaluation, reasons why human resource development (HRD) professionals tend not to conduct evaluations, and an overview of Kirkpatrick's four levels of evaluation.

3. "Evaluation and the Design Process." In this chapter, the focus is on linking evaluation to course design. This chapter also presents criteria for determining the best way to evaluate a course and establishes the evaluation plan.

4. "Level 1: Audience Reaction." After gaining an understanding of what level 1 evaluation is and how the information can be used, the chapter presents common errors and ways to improve level 1 evaluations.

5. "Level 2: Learning and Application During Training." This chapter discusses what is included in a level 2 evaluation, various aspects of testing and other assessments to measure learning and practice, and instructional strategies to support level 2 evaluation.

6. "Level 3: Transfer to the Job and the Environment." In this chapter, the business case and requirements for transfer are discussed, along with the barriers to transfer, and strategies and instruments to support transfer of the new knowledge and skills to the job. Transfer, in its most basic form, is the idea that what was learned in one situation (training) is now being applied in another situation (on the job).

7. "Level 4: Impact and ROI." This chapter links back to the initial design phase when the business metric was established for the evaluation. Level 4 evaluation reveals the impact (change in the business metric) on the organization due to training. Then, the chapter presents the steps to conducting the ROI evaluation analysis and discusses ways to isolate the effects of training from other variables. Finally, it demonstrates how to calculate an ROI.

8. "Evaluation Biases and Communicating the Results." This chapter begins with a discussion of the various biases that can affect the quality and reliability of your information. The issue of bias cuts across all levels of evaluation. This discussion is followed by an outline of an evaluation report. The chapter concludes with the development of a communication plan. Once the study is complete, the results need to be communicated to appropriate audiences in an acceptable format. The communication plan provides a structure to develop a communication plan for different audiences.

9. "A Final Thought." This chapter begins by revisiting the link between evaluation and design/development. This is followed by a discussion on discussing how you can demonstrate value to your client. The chapter closes by discussing the readiness for conducting a more extensive evaluation of

your training programs. Perhaps your organization is not in a position to undertake ROI evaluation yet but is ready to take the next step in enhancing your evaluation efforts.

In addition to the chapter material, you'll find some additional information in the back matter. Appendix A provides several different evaluation instruments that can help you evaluate facilitators and courseware (regardless of delivery method). The Additional Resources section lists some supplementary reading materials related to evaluation and other aspects of HRD.

Icons to Guide You

What's Inside This Chapter

Each chapter opens with a short summary for your quick reference of what is in that chapter. You can use this section to identify the information in the chapter, and, if you wish, to skip ahead to the material that is most useful.

Think About This

These are helpful tips that you can put in your back pocket to help you throughout the evaluation process.

Basic Rules

These rules cut to the chase. They are unequivocal and important concepts for evaluators.

Noted

This icon flags sections that give you more detail or explanation about a concept or a principle.

Getting It Done

The final section of each chapter supports your ability to take the content of that chapter and apply it to your situation. Sometimes this section contains a list of questions for your reflection, sometimes it is a self-assessment tool, and sometimes it is a list of action steps you can take to enhance your facilitation.

Think About This

Evaluation starts with course design. In the design phase, you must
- identify the business metric—the data changes you will track
- identify measurable learning objectives
- develop and implement an evaluation plan
- plan ways to communicate results.

Let's Go!

Evaluation requires some planning and diligence, but it allows you to make a difference in the quality and value of the learning experiences you provide for your clients as you enhance your credibility. Evaluation allows you to document the value that your programs provide for your organization.

This book presents some theory, but the main intent is to provide practical guidelines, methods, models, and instruments to help you become a more effective evaluator. *Evaluation Basics* will reveal the essentials of planning and implementing an evaluation plan.

So, use what works for you and your organization, and make it happen. Good luck.

Noted

Effective evaluation is the result of both effective design and effective planning. The implementation of the evaluation plan and subsequent analysis requires the support of the designer, facilitator, participants, and management. Therefore, it takes planning and influence as the evaluator interfaces with several individuals—inside and outside the training or HRD function. Although the evaluation plan provides the structure for your evaluation initiative, it takes time and perseverance to complete the analysis and implement the recommendations.

Getting It Done

This chapter provided you a roadmap to *Evaluation Basics* and outlined some ways that the material in this book can help you evaluate your programs in a meaningful way. Now it's time to think about some initial issues and practices regarding evaluation to see where you and your organization are in terms of evaluating programs. Exercise 1-1 can help you structure your thoughts around evaluation.

Exercise 1-1. Are you ready to move ahead with evaluation?

1. The first section of this exercise addresses your organization's current level of evaluation and the readiness to go further in your evaluation efforts. The second section deals with your current evaluation practices. Read each statement and indicate whether your current evaluation practices support the statement (yes) or not (no). You may also indicate "not sure" if you don't have the information to make the decision.

	Yes	No	Not Sure
Organization's Evaluation Readiness			
Clients are asking for more evaluation data.			
Clients and management are involved in the design/development process.			
The organization's culture supports training transfer.			
Client support depends on HRD demonstrating value.			
Client establishes business metric for evaluation measurement.			
Client places a dollar value on the business metric.			
Client supports data collection methods.			
HRD management supports more sophisticated evaluation.			
HRD management wants to use evaluation data for program improvement.			
HRD budget is shrinking.			
Evaluation expertise is on staff or can be contracted.			
Courseware is designed for evaluation.			
There is a current initiative to improve evaluation efforts.			
HRD professionals are held accountable for quality of training.			
There is a willingness to change programs based on evaluation findings.			
Program participants support evaluation efforts.			

	Yes	No	Not Sure
Evaluation Practices			
Course objectives are jointly developed with the client.			
Evaluation is an integral part of the entire design/development process.			
Course objectives are measurable.			
Course objectives are written for level 2 evaluation (knowledge shift and practice application).			
Course objectives are written for level 3 evaluation (transfer and environment).			
Course objectives are written for level 4 evaluation (impact and ROI).			
There is a comprehensive evaluation plan for courses.			
Assessment instruments are developed for each level to be evaluated.			
Evaluation instruments align with the learning objectives.			
Instruments for evaluation level 2 provide for knowledge assessment (pre-test, post-test, in-class).			
Instruments for evaluation level 2 provide for practice/application assessment.			
Instructional strategies support level 3 evaluation.			
Appropriate data collection methods are used for each stage of evaluation.			
Evaluation results are used for program improvement.			
Specific individuals are held accountable for program evaluation.			

2. Based on your initial assessment of *your organization's* evaluation readiness, develop three specific actions to support that readiness or that can help overcome inertia.

Actions:

1.

2.

3.

(continued on page 8)

Exercise 1-1. Are you ready to move ahead with evaluation (continued)?

3. Based on your initial assessment of *your own* evaluation practices, develop three specific actions to enhance those practices.

Actions:

1.

2.

3.

2

An Overview of Evaluation

What's Inside This Chapter

In this chapter, you'll learn:

▶ A basic definition of evaluation
▶ Several purposes and benefits of evaluation
▶ Some reasons why HRD professionals avoid doing evaluation
▶ Roles and responsibilities for evaluation
▶ The basics of the four levels of evaluation.

What Is Evaluation?

When you think of evaluating something, what do you think of? Some things that come to mind include assessing something against certain standards or criteria, determining its usefulness or quality, comparing it against other similar programs or products, and so forth. For example, think of purchasing a car. Many buyers evaluate one vehicle against others. They set up criteria that may include style, cost, gas mileage, safety, reliability, resale value, and other factors. They then evaluate cars against those standards. Through this type of process, they make a decision.

Evaluation of training is similar. The course is evaluated using a standard. The standard is formalized through some sort of instrument so you can consistently evaluate all courses against the same standard. You use the results to make some decision regarding the course design, development, implementation, and impact. Therefore, one idea is that evaluation is measuring something in order to make a decision. The decisions could include stopping or expanding the offering, changing the content or instructional strategies, or using the evaluation results to secure additional funding. So, evaluation can be thought of as a process of appraising training to determine and improve its value. This idea includes measuring the quality of the learning event, the actual learning that has occurred, changes in learners' behavior, application of the new knowledge and skills on the job, and impact on the organization.

Purposes of Evaluation

Gathering data and conducting an analysis only provides information. That information must be used for some purpose. Some of the purposes for conducting evaluation include the following:

> ▶ *To improve the design of the learning experience:* Evaluation can help you verify the needs assessment, learning objectives, instructional strategies, target audience, delivery method and quality of delivery, and course content.

> ▶ *To determine if the objectives of the learning experience were met and to what extent:* The objectives are stated in measurable and specific terms. Evaluation will determine if each stated objective was met. Nevertheless, it is not enough to know only if the objectives were met; you must know the extent to which the objectives were met. This knowledge will allow you to focus your efforts for content reinforcement and improvement.

> ▶ *To determine the adequacy of the content:* How can the content be more job related? Was the content too advanced or not challenging enough? Does all the content support the learning objectives?

> ▶ *To assess the effectiveness and appropriateness of the instructional strategies:* Case studies, tests, exercises, and other instructional strategies must be relevant to the job and reinforce course content. Does the instructional strategy link to a course objective and content? Is it the right instructional strategy to drive the desired learning or practice? Was there enough instruction and feedback? Does it fit with the organization's culture? Instructional strategies, when used as part of evaluation, can measure the knowledge, skills, and abilities the learning experience offers.

▸ *To reinforce learning:* Some evaluation methods can reinforce learning. For example, a test or similar performance assessment can focus on content so that content retention is measured and evaluated. The measurement process itself causes the learner to reflect on the content, select the appropriate content area, and use it in the evaluation process.

▸ *To provide feedback to the facilitator:* Did the facilitator know the content? Did the facilitator stay on topic? Did the facilitator provide added depth and value based on personal experience? Was the facilitator credible? Will you use the evaluation information to improve the skills of the facilitator?

▸ *To determine the appropriate pace and sequence:* Do you need to schedule more or less time for the total learning experience or certain parts of the learning? Were some parts of the learning experience covered too fast or too slowly? Does the flow of the content make sense? Does the sequence follow a building-block approach?

▸ *To provide feedback to participants on learning:* Are the participants learning the course content? Which parts are they not learning? Was there a shift in knowledge and skills? To what extent can the participants demonstrate the desired skills or behavior?

▸ *To identify which participants are experiencing success in the learning experience:* Evaluation can identify which participants are grasping the new knowledge and skills and those who are struggling. Likewise, evaluation can identify participants who are excelling in their understanding of the content and its use on the job.

▸ *To determine business impact, the cost-benefit ratio, and the ROI for the program:* What was the shift in the identified business metric? What part of that shift was attributable to the learning experience? Was the benefit to the organization worth the total cost of providing the learning experience? What is the bottom-line value of the course's impact on the organization?

▸ *To identify the learning that is being used on the job:* What part(s) of the learning experience are being used on the job? To what extent are they being used?

▸ *To assess the on-the-job environment to support learning:* What environmental factors support or inhibit the use of the new knowledge, skills, abilities, and behaviors on the job? These factors could be management support, tools and equipment, recognition and reward, and so on.

▷ *To build relationships with management:* The evaluation process requires an interface with management. The identification of the business metric, the evaluation plan, collection of information, and the communication of results all involve management. This continual interface provides the opportunity to build relationships and add value to the accomplishment of objectives.

▷ *To decide who should participate in this or future programs:* The needs assessment includes an audience analysis. This is one piece of information. In addition, the evaluation will determine the extent to which the content applies to an actual job.

▷ *To gather data for marketing purposes:* Positive results can help promote the learning experience to other potential participants. It can also help position the HRD unit as adding value to internal clients.

As you can see, there are many purposes of evaluation, and the preceding list is not exhaustive. How is this information used? The evaluator determines the purpose of the evaluation as part of the evaluation plan (to be discussed later). This decision then relates to the decisions to be made, the type of data collection instruments, timing, sources, and the location for the data.

Basic Rule 2
The purpose of the evaluation drives the evaluation plan.

Benefits of Evaluation

Implementing the evaluation of learning experiences confers several advantages to the HRD function and to the organization. First, an effective, high-quality evaluation can secure client support and build client relationships. Discussing your evaluation plan demonstrates that you have a structured approach to ensure quality and continuous improvement of your training efforts. This gives the client confidence that his or her investment is well placed.

Second, and in concert with the first benefit, evaluation allows you to see if the results from the learning are consistent with the business opportunity analysis and needs assessment. What contribution did training make to the shift in the business metric? What was the organizational impact?

Third, evaluation helps focus the training. Do you have the right content, directed at the right audience, delivered effectively? The evaluation results provide information regarding the target audience and individual participants. Evaluation also assesses the alignment of the content with the learning objectives, needs assessment data, and the instructional strategies.

Think About This

The purpose behind a specific evaluation plan shapes your evaluation efforts. The purpose constrains and guides your efforts so you don't collect information that does not relate directly to the purpose. Likewise, the purpose is a guide to ensure you are collecting enough information to carry out your evaluation. This tension supports cost-effective evaluation.

Fourth, evaluation validates performance gaps and learner needs. Through various performance measurements (tests, behavioral checklists, action planning, and so forth), you can identify ongoing needs. If a learner cannot perform a skill or pass a test, there is still a gap that needs to be addressed.

Fifth, evaluation can help to determine if training is the solution to a performance gap. Training is generally part of the solution if

- a shift in the business metric occurred
- participants learned and can apply their new knowledge and skills
- the original problem or opportunity was addressed.

Evaluation can also determine if the program was a cost-effective solution. By knowing the total costs of the learning experience and the dollar value of the benefit (from the shift in the business metric), you can determine the ROI. Obviously, a positive ROI is desirable.

Sixth, if you demonstrate value, you may gain access to more resources. Management will fund initiatives that make a difference to it and the organization. By helping management meet its objectives, you have become a partner in that success.

Think About This

If someone asks you, "What is evaluation good for, anyway?" just tell him or her to take a PILL (Eyler, no year):

Proving the value of the program: Demonstrate that the learning experience makes a difference and that the difference is worth the investment. In essence, there is benefit in judging the value of the program.

Improving the value of the program: The improvement may occur in such areas as facilitator delivery or content expertise; materials, facilities, and equipment; program sequence and pace; revision of content and learning strategies.

Linking training to business needs: This goes beyond just identifying a business metric. It involves partnering with management for business unit success. This supports transfer to the job and supports the client in achieving his or her objectives. Therefore, HRD is seen as adding value to the organization.

Learning reinforcement: Some evaluation efforts can serve as course organizers. A pretest can do this. Evaluation also reinforces learning and supports transfer. This means that evaluation and course content focus on outcomes.

So, Why Doesn't Everyone Do Evaluations?

With all these purposes and benefits, it would seem that everyone would be conducting comprehensive evaluations. If only this were true. Many organizations only do the minimum when it comes to evaluation. There are reasons, some more valid than others. Let's take a look at nine reasons why HRD professionals say that they do not evaluate their learning experiences:

1. Evaluation requires a particular skill set. Evaluators must not only know design, but also they must have an intimate knowledge of evaluation. This goes beyond the basics. The evaluator must know data collection methods and have the skills to design instruments, the ability to analyze data, project planning skills, the ability to influence, and strong communication skills.

2. Evaluation is not a priority. Let's face it: Everyone is busy and evaluation does require time and effort. Although many evaluation instruments can be designed into the learning experience, it still takes time to collect, analyze, and report the evaluation results. The issue, then, is really one of priority,

not time. If evaluation were to become a priority, would HRD professionals have the time? The answer is yes.

3. It is not required. In some cases, no one is asking for evaluation. Don't be fooled. Just because no one is asking does not mean that evaluation is not important. Even if HRD is not pushing the envelope in this area, your internal clients are asking the questions. They are results-driven managers with profit-and-loss responsibilities; they want to know if the training is effective.

Basic Rule 3

It is not safe to assume that just because no one is asking for evaluation that no one wants it.

4. It can result in criticism. Evaluation results are communicated to HRD management and the client organization. Because evaluation also takes place during the learning experience, the learners also receive feedback. Evaluation should be seen as efforts for continuous improvement, but it may also result in some criticism. Like all criticism, the receiver of the criticism must look at the source and validity of the comments and act accordingly. In some cases, damage control may be in order. In all cases, criticism can be a catalyst for improvement.

5. You can't measure training. Many in HRD look at training as an investment much like advertising. Investments are made without really knowing the results because they cannot be measured. Or, what can be measured has so many influences that training's contribution to change cannot be separated out from other factors. Much of the problem lies in the fact that a business metric is not determined. Without some change to measure, measurement is not possible.

6. Too many variables are beyond the HRD department's control. The perception is that training's impact cannot be isolated and measured because so many variables affect performance. The thinking is that there is no way to separate all these variables and focus on training. This is a difficult task, but it is not impossible.

7. The information is not available. Do you mean that although the organization has the information, you cannot get the information? Do you mean

that the organization does not have the information? Do you mean that the information is not in a form that can be used for evaluation? Just what does this statement mean? If you work with an internal client to identify a business metric, that client will have the information. He or she most likely has a part of the necessary information as a performance objective. Companies have systems that track a great deal of information. Availability of the data is another issue. You client should open the doors to make the information available if it is important to the evaluation effort.

8. There is no system to track data. If your client has a performance objective that you will help him or her achieve, then the client can track that information. It is true that most companies will not set up a separate system to track a change for a training evaluation effort. Therefore, link to whatever the existing method is to track the data. If someone is accountable for effecting a change, he or she will have a tracking system.

9. It costs too much. Cost always rears its ugly head when undertaking any initiative. Regarding evaluation, there are costs in terms of time—time to develop the instruments and the time to analyze the results and communicate results. If these skill sets do not reside within the organization, you may need to either develop the skills (training costs), hire an evaluator (staffing and personnel costs), or outsource the evaluation (vendor/consulting costs). You must also consider the opportunity costs of the forgone benefits that could have derived from other uses of the time and dollars spent on the initiative.

Think About This

There are always costs for any initiative; it is a matter of tradeoffs. Evaluation costs time and money, but consider the costs in terms of dollars for staff time, reputation, funding, individual and organizational performance, and so on for training programs that are not effective. Evaluation can help you avoid wasting precious resources on programs that don't work and focus on the programs that do work.

As you can see, the reasons for not evaluating learning experiences may not be as valid as first thought. If you run up against some of these reasons, push back and test the thinking. Do a little investigation to see if the reason is valid or if it is based on faulty thinking and perceptions.

Think About This

The identification of a business metric (sales, turnover, defects, grievances, and so forth) is critical to evaluation. Just as critical is the identification of an internal client who owns the business metric and has it as a performance objective. Internal clients provide access to people and information critical to data tracking and collection. Involve the client in the evaluation planning and get his or her support.

Roles and Responsibilities for Evaluation

Evaluation is not just the responsibility of the course designer, facilitator, or evaluator. Although the training organization takes the lead, the client, the participants' managers, and the participants themselves also have responsibilities to ensure a complete evaluation. The following is a discussion of roles and responsibilities regarding training evaluation.

Training Organization

Regarding evaluation, the HRD department is responsible for

- working with the client to identify the business metric and to complete the evaluation plan
- designing data collection instruments and collecting and interpreting data
- implementing the evaluation plan
- designing a learning experience that can be evaluated beyond level 1
- developing learning experiences that have evaluation design, principles, procedures, strategies, and instruments in place to measure results
- facilitating the training to ensure learning and transfer

- implementing the evaluation plan, instructional strategies, and measurement instruments before, during, and after the learning experience
- communicating the evaluation results to appropriate audiences
- using the evaluation data for making decisions according to the evaluation plan
- following up to ensure decisions based on the evaluation plan are implemented.

Client

As you can see, HRD professionals have a great deal to do in evaluating training. To be successful, they must partner with the client, whose responsibilities include

- working with the HRD professional in identifying the business metric and developing the evaluation plan
- ensuring that a tracking mechanism is in place to monitor the change in the business metric
- providing access to people and data to support the evaluation plan
- being actively involved in the design/development process
- offering input and support to ensure that the training links to the business needs, the content is relevant to the participants' jobs, instructional strategies and assessments are job related and consistent with the culture, and training is directed to the appropriate audience.

Participants' Managers

The managers or supervisors of the participants have important responsibilities regarding evaluation. To support the evaluation effort, they should

- identify employees whose participation in the learning experience is critical for the desired business improvement
- work with the HRD professional to complete an audience profile
- participate in the needs assessment, design process, and curriculum development
- make the participant, other individuals, and data available to the evaluator after the training
- support the data collection efforts.

As with the client, managers need to be actively involved in the design/development process.

Participants

Participants cannot escape responsibility for being a part of the evaluation effort. They can contribute to the evaluation process by

- participating fully in the learning experience, including performing their best regarding instructional strategies, tests, and other assessments
- partnering with their managers to choose learning experiences intended to improve individual and business performance
- applying the new knowledge, skills, and abilities to the job
- providing feedback on the learning experience and environment
- working with their managers to remove barriers to fulfill the evaluation plan
- supporting the posttraining data collection effort
- completing all evaluation instruments and submitting them on time.

Of course, the client and the participants' managers also have responsibilities for the learning and transfer processes, without which training cannot be effective. Some of these responsibilities include

- ensuring that the required systems and processes are in place to support learning and transfer
- identifying employees whose participation in the learning experience is critical for the desired business improvement
- developing and sustaining an environment conducive for learning and transfer, including opportunities and support for the use of the new knowledge, skills, and abilities on the job
- providing the required resources before, during, and after the training to support the participant's learning and application of the new knowledge, skills, and abilities on the job
- discussing the learning experience with participants prior to their participation to determine expected outcomes, explain the transfer of learning to the job, and complete the performance contract
- reinforcing behavior after the learning experience and providing rewards and recognition for success
- being proactive in identifying and removing barriers to application of the new knowledge and skills
- holding learners responsible for using and sharing their learning.

Basic Rule 4

A complete evaluation effort requires the involvement and support of the HRD staff, training participants, managers of the participants, and the client.

Think About This

In many cases, an evaluator must access information that is in the client's database. Therefore, the evaluator needs to work with the people who are the keepers of the data.

Building on the Four Levels of Evaluation

Donald Kirkpatrick (1994) developed what is probably the best-known model for evaluating learning experiences. His model consists of four levels: reaction, learning, behavior, and results. Jack Phillips (1994) then separated the fourth level and came up with a five-level model consisting of reaction, learning, application, business impact, and ROI. This model allows the evaluator to determine just the business impact of a training course, the shift in the business metric. The evaluator can use that business impact data to determine the ROI for the course, thus placing greater emphasis on both business impact and the link to ROI. Using Kirkpatrick's model as a basis, the model presented in *Evaluation Basics* separates three of Kirkpatrick's levels into sub-parts (figure 2-1). This model depicts levels 2, 3, and 4 each as having two parts.

What is the value of separating out the levels? Why this model? As you recall, there are several purposes of evaluation. By separating the levels, you can better focus your evaluation efforts and report the evaluation results on specific areas of interest. Likewise, the model allows you to have a more detailed discussion with your client, including where some assistance is likely to be needed. For example, a client will want the course content to transfer to the job and believes that this is the responsibility of the HRD department. By discussing the second aspect of level 3 (environment), the client realizes that he or she must be involved in the process. The different levels allow the evaluator to better focus the development of data collection instruments and assign responsibilities to more specific areas of the evaluation plan. Next, by providing more definition around these levels, you can better justify the linkage between levels.

Figure 2-1. A four-level model (with subparts) for evaluating learning experiences.

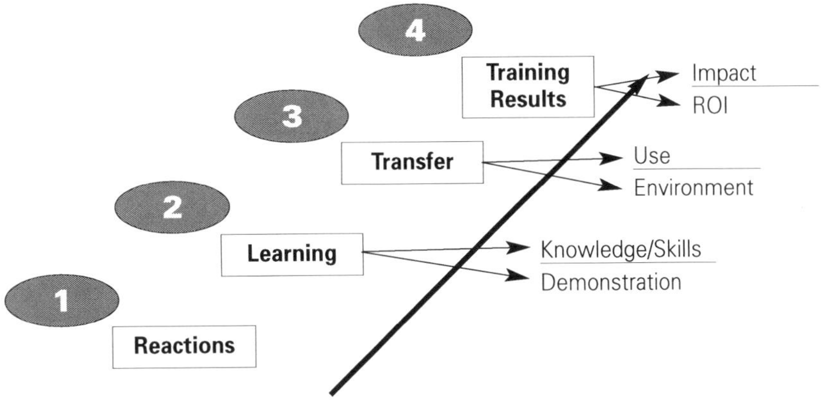

Reprinted with permission from Performance Advantage Group, 2004.

For example, if you are writing an evaluation report on the ROI of a course, you need to incorporate the change in the business metric, the business impact. Likewise, you need to demonstrate not only that the knowledge and skills were used on the job, but also the extent of their use, which directly relates to environmental factors. You will also want to demonstrate that there was not just a shift in knowledge but that the participants could actually demonstrate the application of the knowledge and skills in the training course. So, if the client asks, "How do I know if the use on the job is a result of training?" you can substantiate that the participants could apply the knowledge and skill before returning to the job.

Finally, the models used here can help target where a training problem occurred. For example, if the skills taught in the course are not being used on the job, you will want to prove that the participants could demonstrate those skills in the course. The lack of application may then be related to environmental factors.

Level 1

Level 1 gauges reaction—the participants' immediate response to the learning experience—in much the same way as a customer satisfaction survey does. Level 1 looks at what the participants thought of the learning experience and includes such things as quality of participant materials (usually the pre-reading material and participant guide), facilitator skills (presentation and facilitation skills, management of time and content,

content expertise, ability to "manage" participants), course content and its relevance to the job, facilities, administrative support (registration, information), accuracy of promotional material, and media (varied forms and quality of media). Level 1 is often measured using tools, sometimes called smile sheets, which look like customer satisfaction surveys.

Level 1 provides a first glance at the learning experience. Except for a few areas (changes in the physical environment, administrative support, accuracy of promotional materials), there is not enough information to make changes. Level 1 evaluation gives insights and indicates that more information is needed before making changes.

Level 2

Level 2 has two aspects or parts. The first part is learning. Learning is the extent to which the participants improve their knowledge, skills, and abilities as a result of the learning experience. For level 2, was there a shift in learning? Did learning take place? For example, a diversity or racial awareness program is designed to shift attitudes. Keyboarding, technical training, and computer skills programs are meant to improve skills. Programs involving motivation, leadership, or communication are designed to address all three aspects of learning as they have aspects of knowledge, skill, and attitudes embedded within the learning experience.

Level 2 also addresses the demonstration of the learning within that learning experience. This is the demonstration side of the program content, and is where participants can practice their new skill or behavior. Usually an observer has a checklist to ensure that the demonstration of the new skill or behavior is up to standard. For example, a coaching program teaches the five steps in coaching. For practice, the participants can role-play a coaching session demonstrating the five steps. An observer has an observation feedback (evaluation) instrument. This instrument could be a simple yes/no questionnaire to indicate if the behavior was observed or a scaled instrument to reveal the extent to which the learner demonstrated the five steps of coaching.

Level 3

Level 3 evaluation measures behavior or transfer to the job. The idea of transfer is simply the shifting of something from one place to another. You shift money from savings to checking. Likewise for learning, the knowledge, skills, and abilities gained in the learning experience shift to the work environment and job. This shift is measured in how much the training participants apply the knowledge, skills, and abilities on the job.

Transfer also has two parts. Effective transfer is both a design issue and an environmental issue. The first part is the use of the new knowledge, skills, and abilities on the job. Are the participants now using their learning on the job? To what extent are they using their new learning? Did the learning experience provide them with not only the content for knowledge transfer, but also the skills and tools to apply the course content to their job?

The second aspect of level 3 evaluation is the work environment: the barriers or enablers that support or hinder transfer. For example, one of the barriers to transfer can be the supervisor who prohibits the use the new skills. "We don't do it like that!" is all too common. Another barrier could be timing. Your organization is establishing a new system to become effective January 1. The training on the new system takes place in September. Now, do you really think that the participants will be able to use their new knowledge and skills in several months? A third barrier is the lack of tools or equipment. The equipment or tools that are used as practice in the training are not available on the job. There is also the issue of lack of recognition and reward. The individual goes back to the job and nothing is ever mentioned; the training is not even acknowledged. There is no attempt to provide opportunities for the transfer. There are no new job assignments, sharing of knowledge and skills with peers, praise, or monetary rewards. Nothing! It is business as usual.

However, the environment also can support the transfer process. Some enablers can be incorporated in the design as well as management practices to support learning. The design can include instructional strategies that support transfer. These can be such things as a performance contract, action planning, involvement of management in delivery, and action learning, to mention a few. On the job, the immediate manager can have a discussion incorporating the training in job assignments. The participant can teach peers or do peer coaching, helping others gain knowledge and skills. The manager can ensure that the performance contract or action plans are completed. Verbal praise or a challenging job assignment with exposure to other managers provides recognition. What about a bonus? The challenge for the designer, facilitator, participant, and manager is to create and sustain an environment that enhances the enablers and reduces the barriers to transfer.

Basic Rule 5

The designer, facilitator, participant, and manager all have responsibilities to support transfer.

Level 4

Level 4 evaluation assesses training results and includes both impact and ROI. This is where you go back to the business metric. Did the metric change? Were there fewer grievances or defects? Was turnover reduced? Did sales increase? Did costs decline?

The evaluator must monitor results to measure the impact. After all, the change in the business metric is the reason for the training in the first place. (It will be discussed later if all training results in a measurable impact.) With the impact established, the ROI is a matter of comparing the net impact in dollar terms to the total program costs and expressing the ratio as a percentage:

$$\frac{\text{Program Benefits} - \text{Program Costs}}{\text{Program Costs}} \times 100 = \text{ROI}$$

Very few programs are evaluated using the ROI approach. Even if you do not conduct an ROI analysis, knowing your program costs is important. Knowing program costs can help you manage those costs and deliver a cost-effective learning experience.

 ### Getting It Done

This chapter provided an overview of evaluation. Now, you'll have a chance to apply what you have learned and find ways that you can use evaluation more effectively in your organization. Exercise 2-1 can help you figure out why you or your organization does not conduct evaluation and suggests some ways to overcome this resistance. Exercise 2-2 allows you to rate various types of evaluation activities and develop action plans to implement these types of evaluation measures.

Exercise 2-1. Why don't you evaluate?

Many reasons exist why organizations do not conduct more extensive evaluations. Read the list below and then:

1. Add additional reasons not listed that relate to your organization.
2. In the second column, check the boxes indicating the reasons why your organization does not conduct a more extensive evaluation of the training initiatives.
3. In the third column, note what actions you might take to overcome a particular reason for not evaluating training.

Reason for Not Evaluating	✔	Actions for Overcoming Resistance to Evaluation
Evaluation requires a particular skill set that does not reside in my organization.		
We don't have the time; it's not a priority.		
Evaluation is not required.		
Unfavorable results from evaluation can result in criticism.		
You can't measure training.		
Too many variables are beyond my control.		
The information is not available.		
We don't have a system to track data.		
It costs too much.		

Exercise 2-2. Reasons to evaluate.

Many reasons exist to perform evaluation. Listed below is a list of common reasons for evaluation. Read this list and then:

1. Rate the importance of each evaluation purpose for your organization using the following scale:

> 0 = not important at all
> 1 = of little importance
> 2 = of some importance
> 3 = important
> 4 = very important

2. If you rate an area 2 or less, develop an action plan to increase the importance of that evaluation's purpose for your organization.

Purpose		Action
To improve the design of the learning experience	0 1 2 3 4	
To determine if the objectives of the learning experience were met and to what extent	0 1 2 3 4	
To determine the adequacy of the content	0 1 2 3 4	
To assess the effectiveness and appropriateness of the instructional strategies	0 1 2 3 4	
To reinforce learning	0 1 2 3 4	
To provide feedback to the facilitator	0 1 2 3 4	
To determine the appropriate pace and sequence	0 1 2 3 4	
To provide feedback to participants on learning	0 1 2 3 4	
To identify which participants are experiencing success in the learning experience	0 1 2 3 4	
To determine impact and cost-benefit and ROI	0 1 2 3 4	
To identify the learning that is being used on the job	0 1 2 3 4	
To assess the on-the-job environment for supporting learning	0 1 2 3 4	

Purpose		Action
To build relationships with management	0 1 2 3 4	
To decide who should participate in this or future programs	0 1 2 3 4	
To gather data for marketing purposes	0 1 2 3 4	

Now that you have a basic understanding of evaluation, it is important to understand where and how evaluation fits into the design process. This is the subject of the next chapter.

3

Evaluation and the Design Process

What's Inside This Chapter

In this chapter, you'll learn:

▶ Criteria for course evaluation
▶ Some key design concepts as they relate to evaluation
▶ The integration of evaluation and design
▶ Some advantages and disadvantages of evaluation instruments
▶ How to develop an evaluation plan.

Criteria for Course Evaluation

Can all courses be evaluated? Yes! Can all courses be evaluated at all levels? No. At a minimum, a level 1 evaluation can be implemented for any course. But, for example, if there is no identified business metric for tracking, you cannot establish impact. If the metric cannot be put into dollar terms, then you cannot conduct an ROI evaluation. If no mechanisms are built into the training to assess knowledge or knowledge shift or acquisition of skills, you cannot conduct a level 2 evaluation. This is why evaluation planning and the integration of evaluation into the instructional design process are so important.

That said, some guidelines are available to help you determine whether a training course can be evaluated (or easily evaluated). First, does the program have clear, measurable objectives based on the business analysis and needs assessment? The objectives should be written for both the terminal objectives (what the person should be able to do) and the enabling objectives (what the participant needs to know). Second, is there a logical method to attain those objectives? This criterion encompasses everything from the design/development of the course to management's support to the facilitator's skill to the participant's readiness, and more. Next, is there an evaluation plan with supporting methods, instruments, and responsibilities? (This criterion will be discussed in detail later.) Fourth, do the instructional strategies relate to and support the objectives? The instructional strategies provide for practice and application to the job. There is a direct link among the chosen instructional strategies, the course objectives, and evaluation. Fifth, can the business metric be tracked? If the training is built upon your client's business objectives, data should be available and a tracking mechanism in place. Sixth, can the business metric be converted to a dollar value and can you determine the total costs of the training? This is critical for level 4 evaluation (impact and ROI). Last, do you have access to the field? This is important for data collection to support level 3 evaluation (transfer to the job).

Think About This

The criteria for course evaluation provide guidelines to determine if your course can be effectively evaluated to the desired level. If you cannot answer yes to the questions in the criteria, a red flag should go up. You need to do some planning to ensure that your course can be evaluated.

Key Concepts: Design and Evaluation

Evaluation is not just something you do at the end of a program. Evaluation is part and parcel of the design/development process. Rather, evaluation begins at the front end of the design process (business analysis and needs assessment) and is integrated throughout the entire process.

Basic Rule 6
Evaluation starts at the beginning of instructional design.

Business Opportunity Analysis and Needs Assessment

Evaluation is based on business opportunity analysis and needs assessment. The business opportunity analysis addresses the strategies and goals of the client. What is the client trying to achieve? Is the client trying to increase product sales? Is the client facing a quality problem and seeking to reduce defects or returns? What about turnover? The business analysis identifies the client's issues. You then identify the learning components to the resolution of that issue.

The needs assessment should identify the knowledge, skills, and abilities required to address the business opportunity analysis. The learning is designed to address these needs. Evaluation assesses the extent to which the participants have mastered the knowledge, skills, and abilities; applied them on the job; and the subsequent impact on the organization.

Learning Objectives

Learning objectives are critical for evaluation. Learning objectives are statements of what the participants will be able to do as a result of the training. They should be written in measurable terms. They are supported by statements of what the participants need to know to fulfill the learning objective. Evaluation assesses whether the participant can "do" and whether the participant "knows" related to the objectives.

Specifically, objectives have three components:

▸ *Performance:* what the participant is expected to do and what he or she must know to support the performance
▸ *Standard:* the quality standard indicating acceptable performance
▸ *Conditions:* a statement indicating the conditions under which the participant will apply the new knowledge, skills, and abilities.

Learning objectives describe what the learner must be able to do in order to demonstrate mastery. Here are some examples of learning objectives that state the performance, the standard, and conditions:

▷ Given five overdue credit situations and credit agreements for each situation, calculate the interest to be paid, with no errors.

▷ Given two customer situations, methods of negotiations, and guidelines for negotiating settlements, demonstrate how to negotiate a win-win settlement, staying within guidelines and while using negotiations methods.

▷ Given the tools, repair manual, and a broken laser printer, repair the printer until the printouts are properly aligned, in focus, and in three colors.

Avoid writing overly general objectives. Many such objectives begin with "understand" or "appreciate" or a similar verb. Here is an example of a learning objective that is too general:

▷ The participant will understand the coaching process.

How do you measure "understand"? If you want to measure knowledge, you can ask the participant to list the five steps in the coaching process, or you can state the objective thus:

▷ Given the guidelines for conducting a coaching session, demonstrate an effective coaching session utilizing all the guidelines.

Learning objectives reflect needs assessment, content, instructional strategies, and evaluation. They are derived from the needs assessment and business analysis. They determine what must be included in the program's content and guide the choice of instructional strategies. Finally, learning objectives provide the criteria you evaluate against.

Noted

Learning objectives are written at the level at which you want to evaluate. For example, if your evaluation plan indicates that you will evaluate the learning at level 2, then you must have learning objectives for level 2. Level 2 learning objectives must state what the performer will be able to do and know. For level 3, the objectives indicate what the participant must do on the job.

Business Objectives

The client owns the business objectives that must be met. These were identified in the business opportunity analysis. The client is responsible for implementing strategies and tactics to achieve those objectives. Learning is but one of those strategies. The client then identifies the business metric based on business objectives. The client establishes the value of the metric. The client has the tracking mechanism to see if there is a change.

You will complete the evaluation plan with the client. The client gives input about the extent to which evaluation is necessary for his or her business decisions. The client also helps implement the evaluation plan.

Basic Rule 7
Involving the client is not optional.

Evaluation links training objectives to organizational goals. The organizational goals are the client's business objectives that you are going to help him or her attain through your training and development initiative. By helping the client be successful, you are not only viewed as a partner, but a partner that adds value to the client's business unit. The evaluation effort links the business metric (from the client's objectives) to all four levels of evaluation.

The Integration of Evaluation and Design

The Designing for Impact model (figure 3-1) depicts the major steps of design and development and the role of evaluation at each step. This model depicts the entire process; evaluation-related segments are discussed here in more detail than the others.

As previously discussed, the business opportunity analysis identifies the client's objectives, which then become the business metric for evaluation. Some examples of metrics include product sales figures, turnover rates, number of defects, rework rates, number of grievances, customer satisfaction ratings, customer service level adherence, inventory turns, collection period, and so forth. Stage 1 then compares the current performance to the business objectives to determine the gap. Stage 1 also identifies the knowledge, skills, and abilities required to close the gap.

Figure 3-1. The Designing for Impact model.

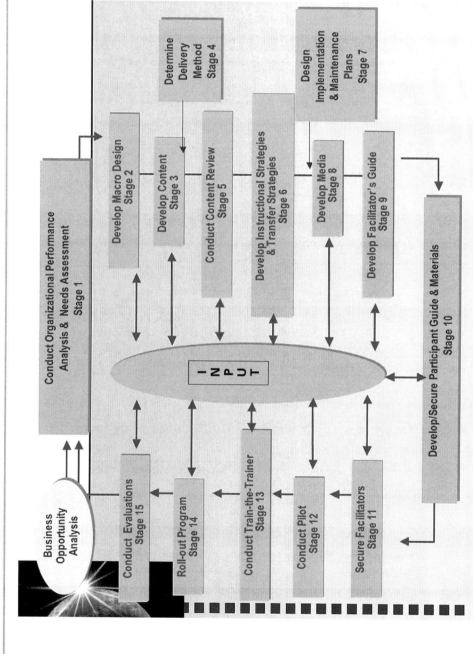

Conduct Organizational Performance Analysis & Needs Assessment
Stage 1

Develop Macro Design
Stage 2

Develop Content
Stage 3

Determine Delivery Method
Stage 4

Conduct Content Review
Stage 5

Develop Instructional Strategies & Transfer Strategies
Stage 6

Design Implementation & Maintenance Plans
Stage 7

Develop Media
Stage 8

Develop Facilitator's Guide
Stage 9

Develop/Secure Participant Guide & Materials
Stage 10

INPUT

Business Opportunity Analysis

Conduct Evaluations
Stage 15

Roll-out Program
Stage 14

Conduct Train-the-Trainer
Stage 13

Conduct Pilot
Stage 12

Secure Facilitators
Stage 11

Think About This

Evaluation is linked to the business analysis and needs assessment and is part of the design. Each level of evaluation is linked to provide a strong case for learning, transfer, and impact.

The macro design, stage 2, is where the course starts to take shape. The activities in the macro design include developing the learning objectives, developing a content outline, identifying initial instructional and transfer strategies (for example, role plays, case studies, action plans, peer teaching, performance contracts), conducting the audience analysis, choosing potential delivery methods, and completing the evaluation plan. Once completed, you discuss the stage 2 work with your client and, if possible, some potential participants and their managers.

Then, the content is fully developed based on the learning objectives and outline (stage 3). The learning objectives determine what content is included (or excluded). Based on the information from the macro design and content, determine the delivery method (stage 4). It could be classroom, self-study, e-learning, blended learning, and so forth. This stage is followed by a content review (stage 5) with the same individuals who provided input for the macro design. This discussion covers the content of the course and the method(s) to deliver the content. You want to verify both for appropriateness of the audience.

With client and participant support, develop the instructional and transfer strategies (stage 6). These should be consistent with the learning objectives and provide for assessment, practice, and application. The instructional strategies can become evaluation methods and tools.

For stages 7 through 10, remember to get continued input from the client and the sample of participants. Not only does this input serve as a basis for continually refining the course, but it also transfers ownership from the design staff to the client organization.

Stage 11 (secure facilitators) is not part of the traditional four levels of evaluation. Nevertheless, you must evaluate facilitators to determine their capabilities and acceptability to the target audience. Appendix A provides a facilitator checklist to assist you with selecting facilitators.

The pilot (stage 12) has an evaluation component to it. The pilot evaluation usually covers levels 1 and 2 by securing extensive feedback. This in-depth information is used for course revisions before rollout, stage 14.

Stage 15 (conduct evaluations) includes the implementation of the evaluation plan and can extend several months after course delivery.

Noted

Continued input from the client and potential learners leads to a learning experience that is relevant to the learners' jobs. As the client and learners provide more input, they take on more ownership and are less likely to resist the course content and more likely to support transfer.

Developing the Evaluation Plan

The evaluation plan provides a structure to guide your thinking about evaluation. Although learning experiences should be designed for learning, transfer, and impact, you will not evaluate all training at all four levels. The extent to which you evaluate any given course depends on several factors. You will conduct a more extensive evaluation under the following conditions:

- The course is expected to be part of a core curriculum and have a long life.
- The training is linked to client's objectives and is important to meet organizational goals.
- The course supports a strategic initiative for the training organization.
- The more a program costs, the more extensive its evaluation should be.
- The training has high visibility with senior management.
- There is a relatively large target audience.
- Data is readily available.
- There is a defined business metric that has a dollar value associated with it.
- Change in performance is measurable.
- Attendance is mandatory for the learners.
- Senior management requests the evaluation.
- Data can be converted easily to monetary value.
- The redesign/development effort necessary to improve the course is not significant.

Noted

The level to which you will evaluate a training course is a decision between the client and the training organization. As a guideline, evaluate to the extent that the client needs the information for decision making; do no more analysis than the client requires.

Figure 3-2 depicts the evaluation plan. Notice that the four levels contain subparts, allowing more discrimination in data collection for decision making. The first area to complete is the business metric section. In the space provided, you indicate the business metric, provided by the client, which the training is to address. Then, for each level, you complete the matrix.

Think About This

The further you evaluate a course (more levels), the more valuable the information but the more difficult, more expensive, and more time consuming it is to get the information. As you move to levels 3 and 4, you have less control over the data collection because the information comes from areas beyond the training course and outside the training organization.

The What and Why Behind Evaluation Levels

For each area of the evaluation plan it is possible to get more information by asking what and why: What do you want to know and why do you want to know it? What and why go hand-in-hand; they are the first two columns in the evaluation plan. The question of what usually pertains to facilitator skills, course content, instructional and transfer strategies, and the course rollout. The question of why relates to the decisions to be made. Table 3-1 offers some examples of what and why for level 1 evaluation. You will likely need to extend the list of what you want to know and why you want to know it (decisions to be made).

Level 1 evaluation (reaction) does give the evaluator insights into possible areas for revision. The training organization would want to get feedback from several deliveries before taking action on many of the findings. For example, you would not

Figure 3-2. The evaluation plan.

Business Metric(s):
(from business analysis)

Level	What	Why	How	Sources	When	Where	Who
1 Reaction							
2 Learning							
Application							
3 On-the-job							
Environment							
4 Impact							
ROI							

Table 3-1. The what and why behind level 1 evaluation.

What Do You Want to Know?	Why Do You Want to Know It?
To what extent were the course objectives met?	Insights for revising content or instructional strategies; assessment of facilitator effectiveness
Was the facilitator effective?	Training for the facilitator; using another facilitator
Was the facilitator credible?	Training for the facilitator; using another facilitator who has more content depth
Did the facilitator promote an environment of learning?	Training for the facilitator; using another facilitator
Was the content relevant to the job?	Insights for possible revision of content
Was the content presented in the appropriate sequence?	Insights for possible revision of content; possible facilitator training
Were the instructional strategies effective?	Revision of instructional strategies
To what extent did the instructional strategies reinforce the content?	Revision of instructional strategies
Did the participant guide or other materials enhance the learning?	Revision of participant materials; change of format
Was the environment conducive to learning?	Change of locations; better facility management
Did the multiple forms of media enhance learning?	Change of media types used
Did the media meet quality expectations?	Improvement to meet expectations
Did the pre-course material prepare participants for the training?	Revision or elimination of pre-course material
Did the participants complete the pre-course assignments?	Elimination of pre-course work; change in timing or delivery method; strategies to ensure completion of the pre-course work

Basic Rule 8

Determine the what and why for the desired evaluation levels before completing the remainder of the evaluation plan for a program.

want to change course content nor redesign the instructional strategies based on the feedback from just one or two deliveries.

The idea is that level 1 only gives insight. Many times trainers make decisions based on level 1 and they should get more information. Level 2 evaluation (learning) has two parts:

- learning
- application or the demonstration of the learning within that learning experience.

Table 3-2 offers some examples of what and why for level 2 evaluation. You will likely need to extend the list of what you want to know and why you want to know it (decisions to be made).

Level 3 (transfer or application) also consists of two parts:

- use on the job
- the environmental factors that support or hinder the use of the new knowledge, skills, or abilities on the job.

Consider some examples of the what and why for level 3 evaluation (table 3-3). You will likely need to extend the list of what you want to know and why you want to know it (decisions to be made).

Table 3-2. The what and why behind level 2 evaluation.

What Do You Want to Know?	Why Do You Want to Know It?
To what extent was there a shift in knowledge?	Facilitator development; test (re)development, revision of content and/or instructional strategies
Did the assessments accurately measure learning?	Redevelopment of assessments
Did the assessments accurately measure the participants' demonstration of the learning?	Redevelopment of assessments; change in participant instructions
Did the training content prepare participants for successful learning?	Redesign/development of content; reanalysis of needs assessment and/or audience
Did the instructional strategies allow for practice and demonstration?	Revision or change of instructional strategies; explanation of instructions by facilitator
Were the behavioral checklists used effectively?	Facilitator training; revision of instruments; improvement in instructions

Table 3-3. The what and why behind level 3 evaluation.

What Do You Want to Know?	Why Do You Want to Know It?
What parts of the course content are being used on the job?	Verification of needs assessment and content; facilitator training or change of facilitators; course design relative to practice and application activities
How is the participant's manager supporting the use of the new knowledge, skills, and abilities on the job?	Learning reinforcement; learner recognition and reward; use of learners as advocates and source of testimonials
How is the participant's manager hindering the use of the new knowledge, skills, and abilities on the job?	Development of strategies for management involvement and support; redesign or development of instructional strategies; assessment of appropriateness of content to the audience
Does the culture support training and development?	Development of strategies for culture change; identification of processes and leader behaviors that inhibit or support transfer; development of ways to relate training to other HR practices as career path; recognition and reward; staffing; job requirements

Level 4 (results) has two parts:

▶ impact as measured by the change in the business metric as a result of training

▶ return-on-investment (ROI).

Consider some examples of the what and why for level 4 evaluation (table 3-4). You will likely need to extend the list of what you want to know and why you want to know it (decisions to be made).

The Chain of Evaluation

Completely develop the evaluation plan to the level at which the course is to be evaluated. For example, it is difficult to demonstrate the impact due to training if you cannot demonstrate that the training (new knowledge, skills, and abilities) is being used on the job. This chain of causality (figure 3-3) is critical to a comprehensive evaluation and to the integrity of the process.

The best way is to measure effectiveness at each level and improve the task accomplishment at each level. In other words, by making your program an effective learning

Table 3-4. The what and why behind level 4 evaluation.

What Do You Want to Know?	Why Do You Want to Know It?
Did the business metric change?	Effectiveness of the training; extent to which client's needs were met; value to the client; course continuance; course redesign/development
How much did the business metric change?	Value for the client; content for a communication plan
What part of the business metric change is attributable to the training?	Isolation of variables to see training's contribution to the impact; cost-benefit analysis; program continuance
Were there other benefits?	Added value for client relationship and communication
What is the ROI?	Program funding and continuance
What are the total costs?	Budgeting; management of the training course; efficient use of resources
What is the cost breakdown?	Better cost management; comparison of vendor costs; reduction of program costs
What is the dollar value of the benefits?	ROI calculation; communication with the client and management

Figure 3-3. The chain of evaluation.

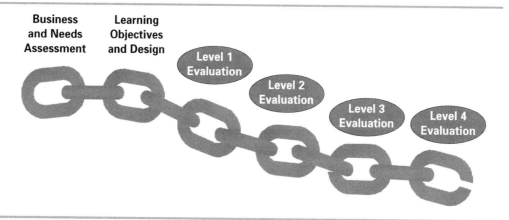

experience at level 1, ensuring that knowledge and skills are mastered at level 2, ensuring that transfer occurs and that the work environment supports application at level 3, you generate the greatest likelihood that the level 4 measures will meet your goals.

The remainder of the evaluation plan indicates how you will gather the required information. "How" (the third column in the evaluation plan, figure 3-2) refers to the methods used to collect the information. Some of the methods are better for one level than another. "Sources" are where you get the information. "When" refers to the timing of the collection of the information for your evaluation. "Where" is the physical location where the information resides. "Who" is the person or people responsible for providing the information.

Figure 3-4 is a completed evaluation plan with some ideas. You will need to align the information with your course and organization.

Noted

Evaluation for levels 3 and 4 is conducted after the training and in the field. The timing is a function of the skill difficulty and the environment. First, the more complex the skills, the longer it would take for a participant to get proficient, that is, the learning curve is longer and requires more reinforcement. Second, you must wait long enough for the environment to take its effect. It is not unusual for participants to go back and start using the new knowledge, skills, and abilities only to run into barriers. So, there must be time to see if there are barriers. Finally, there must be enough time for the business metric to shift. Generally, level 3 evaluation is conducted about three to six months after the training intervention and level 4 evaluation about nine to 12 months after the intervention.

Instruments: Advantages and Disadvantages

The "how" in the evaluation plan refers to the method and instrument used to do the research. When selecting a method or instrument, you should also consider

- the time it takes to develop the instrument and then collect and analyze the information for decisions
- the skills on staff to develop data collection and assessment instruments
- whether the culture supports assessments and evaluation of learning
- the knowledge of the group coming to the training
- how the instrument will be used
- how and to whom feedback will be presented.

Figure 3-4. Example of a completed evaluation plan.

Level	How	Source	When	Where	Who
1	• Questionnaire • Individual in-class responses • Follow-up phone interviews • Checklist	• Participants	• During and after the training	• In the training session	• Course designers and developers • Participants • Facilitator • Evaluator
2 Both Parts	• Knowledge tests • Performance tests on role plays, case studies, simulations, and so forth • Behavioral observation checklists • Product tests • Skill tests	• Participants	• During the training • Pre/post course • After the program	• In the training session • Sometimes in the field	• Course designers and developers • Participants • Facilitator • Evaluator
3 Both Parts	• Monitor performance records • Performance contract • Learning contract • Action plans • Interviews • Focus group • Observation checklist • Questionnaire or survey	• Extant data • Performance review • Performance and learning contracts • Action plans • Participants, peers, and managers of participants	• After the training (a few weeks or three to six months)	• On the job	• Evaluator • Participants • Manager of participants • Peers • Course designers and developers

Level	How	Source	When	Where	Who
4	• Monitor performance records • Track business metric • Monitor performance contract • Monitor learning contract • Monitor action plans • Interviews and focus group • Questionnaire • Use of estimates • Use of control groups • Analyze extant data • Program cost worksheet • Conduct primary and secondary research • Use of trend lines and regression analysis	• Extant data • Performance review • Performance and learning contracts • Action plans • Participants, peers, and managers of participants • External research • Internal or external experts • Professional organizations • External studies • Government • Vendors	• Three to nine months after the training	• On the job	• Evaluator • Participants • Manager of participants • Client • Internal and external experts • Peers • Vendors • Course designers and developers

With the various options available, knowing some advantage and disadvantages of some of the methods can help you decide which instrument to use. Table 3-5 is a good guide.

Table 3-5. Advantages and disadvantages of several data collection instruments

Method	Advantages	Disadvantages
Written Questionnaires	• Relatively fast and easy to administer and calculate results • Can be anonymous: if anonymous, individuals feel free to express their true individual feelings; increases honesty • Relative low cost • Variety of formats • Easily quantified	• Bad reputation as sole tool for measuring reactions • May lack accuracy as individuals hurry to complete it • Questionable rate of return • Requires specific directions • Must be jargon free • Responders determine actual return time
Phone Surveys	• Saves the travel expense associated with interviews • Provides for probing • Once contacted, provides immediate response • Makes a personal contact	• Individuals are difficult to reach by phone • Must develop protocol • Interviewer must be trained • Respondent bias, saying what he/she thinks the interviewer wants to hear • Body language not seen • Respondent may become impatient
Interviews	• Permits individualized give-and-take • Flexible • Interviewers can follow up with questions and thereby probe for information • Trained interviewers improve quality of information • Protocol ensures consistency in format	• Costs, travel expense for field interviews • Can be time consuming • Must have trained interviewers • Labor intensive • Face-to-face interviews may create fear and result in bias information

Method	Advantages	Disadvantages
Focus Groups	• Allows face-to-face discussion and interaction of all learners • Fast • Low cost • Permits group members to obtain ideas from each other • Protocol ensures consistency in format • Good qualitative responses	• Face-to-face discussions allow individuals to dominate the discussion, creating false conclusions that are not representative of a group • Limited in the quantity of information that can be obtained • May be hard to arrange • Hard to summarize and interpret information • Labor intensive • Must have trained leader

Tests	• Can be written or oral
	• Provide written documentation
	• Reinforces content
	• Easy to score
	• Multiple formats
	  —True-False
	  —Multiple-Choice
	  —Matching
	  —Completion
	  —Listing
	  —Essay
		• Difficult to write
		• Some people fear tests
		• Must be part of the course design
		• People worry that test results will become known to others and used inappropriately

Observation	• Can be nonthreatening • Checklist provides consistency • Good measure of change in behavior	• Must develop a checklist • Can be obtrusive • May get biased results • Observer must be trained • Can be threatening
Performance Test	• Reliable • Job related • Objective	• Takes time • Costly • Simulations or instruments difficult to construct
Extant Data or Client/Company Performance Records	• Accepted by client • Objective • Measurable • Can determine dollar value • Organization is tracking the data • Reliable • Job related	• May not be in a usable form • Internal political issues • Access to data • May need to interpret the data • May not be tracked according to your timeline for evaluation

Getting It Done

Here are two activities to help you apply the ideas in this chapter. Recall the guidelines presented in this chapter, which indicate whether a training course can be evaluated or easily evaluated. For exercise 3-1, consider a training course that is either under development or one that you want to evaluate. Then, indicate whether the course meets the guidelines by checking the yes or no box.

For areas where you indicated a response of no, develop actions that can improve your ability to evaluate the training course. Write them in the space provided in the rightmost column of exercise 3-1.

Exercise 3-1. How easy is your program to evaluate?

Guideline	Yes	No	Action to Improve Ability to Evaluate
1. Does the program have clear, measurable objectives based on the business analysis and needs assessment?			
2. Is there a logical method to attain those objectives?			
3. Is there an evaluation plan with supporting methods, instruments, and responsibilities?			
4. Do the instructional strategies relate to and support the objectives?			
5. Can the business metric be tracked?			
6. Can the business metric be converted to a dollar value and can you determine the total costs of the training?			
7. Do you have access to the field?			

Next, try your hand at developing an evaluation plan for one of your courses under development (exercise 3-2). Start by identifying in conjunction with your client the business metric the training is to address. With your client, jointly determine the level

Exercise 3-2. Develop an evaluation plan for one of your programs.

Business Metric(s):
(from business analysis)

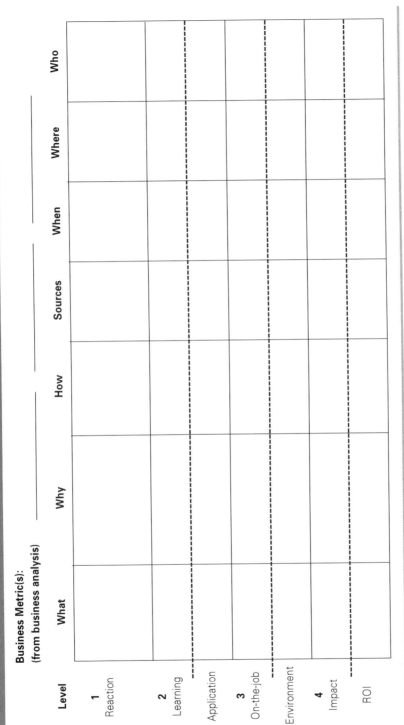

Level	What	Why	How	Sources	When	Where	Who
1 Reaction							
2 Learning							
Application							
3 On-the-job							
Environment							
4 Impact							
ROI							

Reprinted with permission from Performance Advantage Group, 2004.

to which the course will be evaluated. For some hints, look back at figure 3-4 and tables from earlier in the chapter.

This chapter looked at the integration between design and evaluation and developed an evaluation plan for each of the four levels. The following chapters look at each level in some detail. Chapter 4 goes into depth on several aspects of level 1 evaluation.

4

Level 1:
Audience Reaction

- -

What's Inside This Chapter

In this chapter, you'll learn:

- ▶ A working definition of level 1 evaluation
- ▶ Reasons for conducting level 1 evaluations
- ▶ The importance of conducting level 1 evaluation
- ▶ What level 1 evaluation includes and what it excludes
- ▶ Guidelines for conducting level 1 evaluation
- ▶ Common errors in level 1 evaluation
- ▶ Ways to improve level 1 evaluation.

Defining Level 1 Evaluation

Level 1 evaluation is the measure of participants' reaction to the training. It is like a customer satisfaction measure because it involves collecting subjective perceptions and feelings of the participants. The areas evaluated provide indicators of the effectiveness of such things as the participants' perception of the degree to which program objectives were met, pace and sequence, quality of media, appropriateness of content, facilitator knowledge and skill, quality of participant materials, quality and variety of media, and the effectiveness of instructional strategies. Level 1 is usually done immediately following a learning experience, though sometimes it is done during and after the training.

Reasons for Conducting Level 1 Evaluations

There are several reasons for conducting level 1 evaluations. First, level 1 provides feedback to training staff to improve the program by identifying specific problem areas. In reality, you only get insights into areas for program improvement. You would want to do more extensive evaluation before launching into course redesign, though. That said, level 1 evaluation provides excellent indicators regarding achievement of objectives, pace and sequence, job relevancy, learning environment, materials, and so forth.

Level 1 evaluation provides quantitative feedback to managers and clients about learners' reactions to the program. Most level 1 evaluations are scaled-survey instruments providing data that can be quantified. Level 1 may be the basis for conversations between a client and the training department about such areas as the quality of facilitation, media, and materials; whether the content aligns with the job; and logistical issues.

Additionally, level 1 provides measurements for standards of acceptable training performance. For example, you could have a performance standard that the training courses need to receive an average score on level 1 evaluation of 4.5 on a five-point Likert scale (with 1 being low). Or, facilitators may have a performance standard related to the quality of their facilitation based on participant feedback on a level 1 evaluation.

Noted

Who is really interested in the various levels of evaluation? Levels 1 and 2 are for the facilitator, the designer, and their managers because the results of level 1 are used in making initial decisions for course improvement—but not for personnel decisions. Level 3 is for all: the facilitator, the facilitator's manager, and the client for continuing course improvement on transfer and the job environment factors. Level 4 evaluation is for HRD management and the client.

Level 1 evaluation provides a vehicle for participants to give immediate feedback to the training organization. As data is collected, summarized, and analyzed, the training organization gets a picture showing how well its training and services are being received by the organization.

Finally, level 1 evaluation links to other levels of evaluation. It is the first of the four levels, each of which builds on the next. For example, it is important for the training organization to know if the course objectives are being met (from the participant's perspective) and if the course content is job related. This supports evaluation at the other levels for learning, transfer, and impact.

Level 1: What It Includes and Excludes

Many, many, many training organizations, regardless of size, conduct level 1 evaluation. Although it is relatively simple and fast, it is not intended to be extensive. Oftentimes trainers want to use level 1 evaluation as a basis for making decisions regarding areas that the instrument and process were not designed to measure. This is a misuse of evaluation. Table 4-1 summarizes what level 1 evaluation includes and excludes.

Basic Rule 9
If you aren't going to use the information, don't ask the question.

Noted

Include only areas in the evaluation where feedback is needed for reinforcement or change. Sometimes level 1 questions are asked about areas where it isn't feasible to achieve any change. For example, many times the learning facilities are corporate facilities or those under contract. Maybe the level 1 evaluation points out problems with the room's lighting, chairs, or acoustics. There's probably little or nothing you can do about these issues that learners have raised. Therefore, you need to make a decision about whether to include a section on facilities on your level 1 instrument. If you don't have any input or control over the facilities, why raise the expectation that something may change?

Table 4-1. Level 1: What's included and excluded?

Level 1 Evaluation Includes:	Level 1 Evaluation Excludes:
• The quality, relevance, and completeness of participant materials • The extent to which the stated objectives were met • Quality of facilitation • Facilitator acceptance (credibility to the audience) • Quality and appropriateness of instructional methodology (role plays, case studies, reflection, group work, and so forth) • Effectiveness of sequence of material (for example, from general to specific; building-block fashion, from known to unknown; from easy to difficult) • Appropriateness of pace of the course • Quality and variety of media to support the learning • Facilities relative to supporting the learning environment • Relevance of course content to the job • Learners' intent to apply the content on the job	• Specific measures of learning or practice • Assessment of on-the-job performance • Evaluation of environmental factors related to transfer • An assessment of the impact on the organization and ROI • Training costs • Actual application to the job

Think About This

Sometimes trainers conduct a level 1 evaluation on programs that are ongoing and are not going to be changed. Carrying out such evaluations is just a habit. The trainer or evaluator collects the information, gives it a cursory glance, and then files it. Think about other options, such as not conducting the evaluation in the first place or just doing it on a random sample basis.

Advantages of Level 1 Evaluation

There are several advantages to conducting a level 1 evaluation, including the following:

▶ It is a very familiar approach. If you are not conducting any evaluations, this is an easy one to start with. Many models are available that can be used off the shelf or adapted to your program. One model is presented later in this chapter.

▶ They can be built into the training program, reducing delivery and retrieval time.

▶ They are easy to construct and tabulate.

▶ The information is quantifiable.

▶ Participants don't feel intimidated because they are providing anonymous feedback on unthreatening topics.

▶ They provide immediate feedback to the facilitator and training organization.

Disadvantages of Level 1 Evaluation

There are also some weaknesses associated with level 1 evaluation. First, although the information can be quantified, it is still subjective. You are asking the participants their opinions on certain aspects of the course. Second, the participants may not be the best judges. Just because a participant does not like doing case studies or group work does not mean that the instructional strategy is the wrong strategy. Next, minor issues may disproportionately affect some ratings. For example, if the participants liked the facilitator, the entire course may receive a high rating. Or, the participant may disagree with some content or other participants, thereby negatively impacting the ratings.

Finally, the evaluation may drive the wrong behavior on the part of the facilitator. Say, for example, that a facilitator has a performance objective regarding his or her quality of facilitation. The level 1 evaluation is the instrument used for measuring performance. To obtain favorable ratings, the facilitator could do any of the following:

▶ avoid addressing behavioral issues in the training program

▶ provide more entertainment than content

▶ fail to correct participants' responses when they are wrong

▶ discard unfavorable evaluations.

Guidelines for Level 1 Evaluation

There are several guidelines for developing and conducting level 1 evaluation, including the following:

▶ Determine what you want to know and why to frame the extent and purpose for the evaluation.

▶ Complete the evaluation plan for level 1.

▶ Develop instruments to secure the information required in the evaluation plan.

▷ Involve key individuals—the designer, participants, facilitator, HRD managers—in the development of the instruments because these people play important roles in deploying the instruments and implementing the findings from the research.

▷ Decide to whom and how the results will be communicated. Will the results be shared with participants, participants' managers, internal clients, or the training organization? Will they be shared at all? In many cases, the facilitator takes a cursory look and gives the results to the training organization. Then, someone tabulates the results and files them. At a minimum, the facilitator and course designer need to see the results.

▷ Design the instruments for ease of data collection and tabulation. Will you use a survey? This is generally what is done. Will it be hard copy or online? Will it provide for scaled responses or yes/no? Will you have open-ended questions? Open-ended questions provide insight but can be hard to interpret and summarize.

Noted

Level 1 instruments often use a four- or five-point Likert scale for participants' responses. Usually the highest number corresponds to a response of "excellent" or "to a very great extent." A score of 0 or 1 is "low" or "not at all." A four-point scale removes the middle neutral value, forcing the respondent to make a choice. Be sure the wording of the survey is consistent with the scale. Also, don't switch scales within a survey. For example, don't begin the survey asking for ratings of poor to excellent and then switch to ratings of "to what extent."

▷ Keep the responses anonymous to ensure that participants provide candid responses. You may want to make a signature optional in case the person wants you to follow up on any of his or her comments.

▷ Consider whether you need to collect demographic data on position, tenure, job classification, and so forth. How is this information going to be used?

▷ Provide the opportunity for additional comments. Although harder to summarize and interpret, allowing participants to explain their thinking can provide high-quality feedback. You need to be selective regarding the areas you want to solicit written comments. Usually, the comment section is at the end

Think About This

Use one consistent scale within the survey. Some level 1 instruments have a Likert scale and a yes/no scale. Others have a scale of 1–5, with 1 being low initially but later shift to 1 being high. Some designers change the scale within an instrument out of the misguided notion that they want to see if the participants are paying attention. In all likelihood, they aren't. Be consistent with the format and scales within the instrument.

of the survey and asks the participant for ideas for improvement. Comments can also be captured as part of each section within the survey.

▶ Link level 1 evaluation to higher levels of evaluation. In your level 1 evaluation, you can probe for the extent learning took place, use on the job, environmental factors, intent to apply, and perceived value/impact to the organization. This can be done by adding statements (degree of agreement) like these:

— I anticipate sharing my learning with my staff.
— I plan to implement relevant sections of my action plan.
— I will receive the necessary support to implement my action plan.
— There are no serious barriers to implementing my action plan.
— If your action plans are implemented, what are the benefits (impact) to the organization? _____
— What would be the approximate dollar value of those benefits? $_____

Noted

If you have a place for comments, ask focused questions. For example, if you just ask about ideas for improvement, you might elicit feedback on everything ranging from breaks (length, how many, food and beverages), to the facilities, to comments about other participants, to course content, to the facilitator, and so on. Again, ask what you what to know. If you want input on course content, ask specifically for comments on course content. This approach helps narrow the responses and provides more useable information. You can then look for consistent comments around the issue you raised.

An Example of Level 1 Evaluation

Figure 4-1 provides an example of a fairly comprehensive level 1 evaluation instrument. This example would need to be customized to a particular course and organization. There are some areas that you would not want or need to include.

Several items merit special attention. First, notice that there are six main areas, each with its own headings. This not only makes it easier for the participant to provide more focused reactions, but also it allows the evaluator to focus on particular areas of interest. Second, there is a place for comments following each section. Although this permits plenty of input, it is also more difficult to summarize results. Third, there is a section for course information to allow the evaluator to analyze the reactions by job classification, session, and location. By looking for consistencies and inconsistencies across these areas, the evaluator can isolate success factors and problem areas. Fourth, the rating scale is 1 to 4, with no middle value. This forces the rater to make a decision and eliminates the central tendency bias. Providing the rating numbers in each area makes is easier for the participant. Ideally, you would put the explanation over each column with a numeric value. Fifth, the objectives for the course are itemized and specific rather than a single item as if all course objectives were met. This allows the evaluator to focus in on course areas that may need changing related to content or facilitator emphasis. Next, the summary section provides an overview of the total reaction to the learning experience. Asking if participants would recommend the course to their peers gives insight into their view of the real value of the course. Last, it is a good idea to thank the person for their willingness to share their reactions.

Basic Rule 10
Customize off-the-shelf evaluation instruments to meet your needs and those of your organization.

Common Errors in Level 1 Evaluation

Level 1 evaluations are so commonplace that many times their importance is overlooked. Because they are so often used, it is easy to overlook some errors.

One error is using the same reaction instrument for all your training courses. Although "recycling" instruments is efficient, it may not provide the detail needed for decision making. In addition, if the participants see the same instrument again and again, they are less likely to give thoughtful responses. Consider customizing at

Figure 4-1. A model for level 1 evaluation.

[Name of Organization]
Course and Facilitator Evaluation

I. Course Information:

Course Title _____   Course #
Course Start Date _____   Session Location:
Worksite Location _____   Job Classification: Admin. Prof. Mgr. Other

The statements below concern specific aspects of this course. Please indicate to what extent you agree with each statement by circling the appropriate number. Please use the following scale:

    1 = Strongly Disagree   3 = Agree
    2 = Disagree   4 = Strongly Agree

II. Course Content:

1	Objectives were clearly explained	1	2	3	4
2	Objectives stated were met				
	Objective 1	1	2	3	4
	Objective 2	1	2	3	4
	Objective 3	1	2	3	4
3	Content is relevant to my job (if not, please explain)	1	2	3	4

Comments:

_____

_____

_____

III. Course Methodology

The following activities/materials helped me understand the course content and achieve the course objectives.

4	Pre-course material received prior to class	1	2	3	4
5	Participants' workbook	1	2	3	4
6	Class discussions	1	2	3	4
7	Exercises and/or activities	1	2	3	4
8	Readings	1	2	3	4
9	Written assignments and/or homework	1	2	3	4
10	Audiovisuals (flipcharts, videos, audiotapes, and so forth)				

Comments:

_____

_____

_____

(continued on page 60)

Figure 4-1. A model for level 1 evaluation (continued).

IV. Instructor/Facilitator

11	Promoted an environment of learning	1	2	3	4
12	Presented content clearly to assist my understanding	1	2	3	4
13	Appeared knowledgeable of the subject matter	1	2	3	4
14	Provided feedback effectively to participants	1	2	3	4
15	Presented content in an appropriate sequence	1	2	3	4
16	Promoted participant discussion and involvement	1	2	3	4
17	Kept the discussion on topic and activities on track				

Comments:

_____

_____

_____

V. Environment/Course Administration

18	The classroom was arranged to facilitate learning	1	2	3	4
19	The class was free of external distractions	1	2	3	4
20	The room was neat and clean	1	2	3	4
21	The information in the course catalog was helpful	1	2	3	4
22	The course description in the course catalog was informative	1	2	3	4
23	The registration process was effective	1	2	3	4
24	I received my pre-course information in time to complete it prior to the course	1	2	3	4

Comments:

_____

_____

_____

VI. Summary

25. Overall rating for the course (✓)

_____ Poor   _____ Fair   _____ Good   _____ Excellent

Comments:

_____

_____

_____

26. Would you recommend this course to your peers?   _____ Yes   _____ No

Please explain:

_____

_____

_____

27. How likely are you to apply this course back on the job? (✓)

____ not at all   ____ somewhat likely   ____ very likely

Which parts of the course are you most likely to apply on the job?

_____

_____

_____

28. Please share with us any information you believe would help us improve the course.

_____

_____

_____

Thank you for taking the time to share your comments and reactions to your learning experience.

least the learning objectives portion of the instruments. These indicate what the persons should be able to do and what they need to know. These vary by course and need to be specifically addressed. A general statement regarding the accomplishment of all objectives does not provide the detail to support the what and why of the evaluation plan for decision making.

A second common mistake is creating an instrument that has only open-ended questions. This type of instrument is difficult and time consuming to analyze and subject to the interpretation of the evaluator. The participants are less likely to complete an instrument that requires a great deal of their time and effort.

Third, sometimes there is a lack of balance in asking positive questions and asking for criticism. If the instrument is skewed one way or another, it is likely to affect the nature of the responses and introduce bias into the results.

Fourth, too often evaluators fail to seize the opportunity to ask questions that link to subsequent, higher-level evaluations. Similarly, there is a temptation to ask needs assessment related questions on a level 1 instrument. For example, at the end of the instrument, a section is added asking participants what other training courses they feel they need. Resist this temptation. At best, the participant will provide global answers that generally do not link to business objectives.

Fifth, evaluators sometimes don't bother to conduct field tests of their level 1 instruments. You want to get input on a draft copy of the evaluation instrument by getting input from the participants before incorporating the instrument into the course for a pilot test. (The pilot test involves actually delivering the course to an audience for the first time and then making revisions.)

Sixth, it is a mistake to not provide feedback to interested parties. Once the data is gathered, analyzed, and decisions made, communicate the findings to appropriate people, who may include the facilitator, the course designer, your manager, and your client.

Last, but not least, evaluators are often guilty of not allowing enough time for participants to complete the survey. Perhaps you're behind schedule and frantically trying to get through the content. Then, during the last few minutes, you ask the learners to complete the survey (getting marginal results by quality and responses), or you ask them to send it back (getting a minimal response rate). If level 1 evaluation is important, plan for it as you would any other activity.

Basic Rule 11

Always field test your evaluation instruments and provide timely, appropriate feedback to key individuals.

Think About This

Hand out the level 1 evaluation instrument before the end of class. Allow sufficient time for participants to complete the evaluation. Handing it out at the last minute does not provide enough time and gives the impression that it is not important. The level 1 instrument can be given out at the last break before the end of the program, the morning of the last day, or even have it included in the participants' manual.

Improving Level 1 Evaluation

Increasingly important in organizations is the measurement of the effectiveness of training programs. Evaluation is an organization's way of determining the value of a course offering and discerning ways to improve a program. You should be continuously analyzing and improving your evaluation processes. In the case of level 1 (reaction, smile sheets), the value can be improved.

Although it takes additional effort, you can get participants' input before the course offering. Prior to the delivery of the program, you can involve participants in the process by having them weight the objectives important to them. This provides input to the facilitators for real-time program adjustment. At the conclusion of the program, participants indicate the extent to which their weighted objectives were met.

In many cases, evaluation stops at the first level. The instrument does provide some insight into the course, and some limited decisions can be made based on the information. As they are used currently, however, it would be difficult to make course content decisions based on most smile sheets.

Steps to Improve Level 1 Smile Sheets

An important area of the reaction evaluation is the degree to which the course objectives are met. After all, the objectives indicate the knowledge to be gained, the skills to be acquired, and the behavior/attitude change desired. The objectives also provide the framework for content development. Involving participants prior to their participation in a delivery by sending out the objectives for their review and input will add significant value to the reaction evaluation or smile sheets. The process involves the four steps outlined here.

Step One

To add value to the evaluation and provide pre-course input to the facilitator, separate the objectives section from the rest of the evaluation instrument. To allow for anonymity, create a separate instruction page and provide a space for the participant's name, position, and business unit. This will allow the facilitator to return the objectives to the appropriate participant at the end of the course.

Attach the instructions and then send the objectives to the participants with their pre-course reading materials. The course objectives are printed on a structured form to allow for participants' input and the weighting of objectives. Ask the participants to prioritize the learning objectives by spreading 100 points among the objectives. If they have additional objectives, they should be added to the list of objectives and weighted. In the examples shown in figure 4-2, you can see that the participant added an objective and provided the weights for all objectives.

Encourage the participants to discuss the course objectives, their additional objective(s), and the weighting of those objectives with their manager. This will begin a dialogue between the manager and participant concerning the course and desired outcomes. In most cases, you'll need to rewrite the input to make the participants' objectives more measurable.

Figure 4-2. Example of a form to collect participant input on course objectives.

Objectives: The Participant Will Be Able to:	Weight	Degree Met	Total
• Describe three learning organization techniques.	10		
• Using format provided, identify four drivers and four restraining forces applicable to moving toward a learning organization.	35		
• Using format provided, develop six individual tactics that will support the drivers or reduce or eliminate the restraining forces identified.	35		
Additional Participant Objectives			
• Identify four keys issues concerning the capture, storage, retrieval, and transfer of corporate intellect.	20		
•			
•			
Course Totals	**100**		**?/400**

The goals of this step are to:

1. Communicate in advance the course objectives to the participants.
2. Secure participant pre-course input into the course objectives.
3. Involve the participants' managers in the process.
4. Bolster the facilitator's understanding about the importance of the objectives to the participants.

Step Two

The objectives with the cover instruction sheet are returned to the facilitator prior to course delivery. By studying the participants' input, the facilitator gets an idea of the participants' priorities and interest in regard to a given objective. This gives the facilitator time to react to any of the participants' input that could affect course emphasis or content.

Based on the participants' input, the facilitator has at least three options:

▷ adjust the emphasis of that particular offering to the class
▷ postpone the course while the content is revised to reflect participants' desire to address additional but similar objectives as is sometimes the case if there

has not been an adequate needs assessment or if the course has been offered for a number of years without revision
▷ deliver the course without revision but try to make adjustments as the program is delivered.

Step Three

At the beginning of the course, the facilitator should address the new objectives provided by participants, emphasizing his or her responsiveness to the participants' needs. Participants' suggested objectives that are not included should also be discussed. The facilitator will want to provide a rationale for not including the objectives and, if possible, provide direction to other programs or readings that may meet their needs.

Step Four

At the conclusion of the course, return all objectives to the individuals with the remainder of the evaluation instrument. The participants are then asked to rate on a scale of 1 to 4 (in this example) the degree to which the objectives were met (figure 4-3).

Figure 4-3. The objectives at the end of the program.

Objectives: The Participant Will Be Able to:	Weight	Degree Met	Total
• Describe three learning organization techniques.	10	4	40
• Using format provided, identify four drivers and four restraining forces applicable to moving toward a learning organization.	35	3	105
• Using format provided, develop six individual tactics that will support the drivers or reduce or eliminate the restraining forces identified.	35	2	70
Additional Participant Objectives			
• Identify four keys issues concerning the capture, storage, retrieval, and transfer of corporate intellect.	20	3	60
•			
•			
Course Totals	**100**		**275/400**

After multiplying the initial weight by the degree met, the result is a weighted average of learning objectives met. (This becomes a scale of 0–400.) Obviously, you can adjust the scale to meet your preference. Each training organization needs to determine what an acceptable score is. In the example in figure 4-3, the final rating is 275/400 (68.75 percent), indicating the overall quality of the course as it relates to the objectives from one participant's perspective.

Advantages and Disadvantages

This approach to the smile sheet

- gives the participants an opportunity to have input into the course learning objectives and content
- provides the facilitator with early input regarding where the interest of the class is for any given objective or new objective(s)
- allows the facilitator the opportunity to tailor the course to meet the needs and interests of the participants
- provides the evaluator, designer/developer, and facilitator with more accurate evaluation information for course revisions
- supports adult learning principles
- facilitates an early discussion between the participant and his or her manager.

Noted

Use the smile sheet as a basis for course revisions. Based on the scores and participant weights for any given objective, you can revise the course by going back and looking at the content and instructional strategies that were driving the accomplishment of those objectives.

This process for using smile sheets is, of course, more time consuming and resource intensive than simply handing out a standard reaction sheet. You'll be creating an expectation that new objectives will be addressed in the course. This could cause more front-end work. The old axiom "If you ask, be ready to respond" applies. Finally, this approach assumes the participant has some knowledge of the course content and direction and his or her individual needs.

Noted

The intent is not to redevelop a course for every delivery. In many instances, the participant's objectives have been covered already in the course content. They are seeking a level of detail that the initial course objectives do not communicate. In this case where the content is in the course, the facilitator merely needs to emphasize that area. In some cases, the facilitator cannot accommodate the objectives of the participant, but whenever possible and with a little effort, you can add significant value to the participants' learning experience.

Getting It Done

This chapter defined and explained the importance of level 1 evaluation. It provided some guidelines and examples, and gave you some ideas about how to improve level 1 evaluation.

Now, imagine that you have a new course you are developing and you're thinking about level 1 evaluation. Using exercise 4-1 as a template, try developing an evaluation plan to capture level 1 data.

Exercise 4-1. Complete a level 1 evaluation plan.

Evaluation Plan: Level 1 (Reaction)

Business Metric(s): _____

Level 1 Reaction	What	Why	How	Sources	When	Where	Who

Using figure 4-1 as a model and working on a separate piece of paper, develop a level 1 evaluation instrument for a course that you have under development.

Having built an evaluation plan and completed level 1 (reaction), you are now ready to evaluate the course for learning and practice. The next chapter takes an in-depth look at level 2 evaluation with an emphasis on developing tests and assessments.

5

Level 2:
Learning and Application
During Training

■ ■

 What's Inside This Chapter

In this chapter, you'll learn:

▶ A working definition of level 2 evaluation
▶ The importance of level 2 evaluation
▶ What level 2 includes and what it excludes
▶ Advantages and disadvantages of level 2 evaluation
▶ Guidelines for level 2 evaluation
▶ Development and implementation of tests
▶ Types of level 2 assessments.

Defining Level 2 Evaluation

Level 2 evaluation of learning is the process of collecting, analyzing, summarizing, reporting, and applying information to assess how much the participants learned in a program and how well they can apply their new knowledge, skills, and abilities in the context of the learning experience.

Level 2 has two aspects or parts. The first part is learning—the shift in participants' knowledge, skills, and behaviors. The second part is the demonstration of the learning within that learning experience. This is how participants are assessed on the practice of their new skill or behavior. Therefore, the purposes of a level 2 evaluation are to determine if the participant:

- acquired new knowledge
- acquired a new skill or improved an existing skill
- had a change in attitude within the learning experience
- changed his or her behavior within the learning experience.

Reasons for Conducting Level 2 Evaluation

Level 2 evaluation provides a higher quality of feedback for decision making than level 1 does. First, level 2 evaluation can provide feedback to the facilitator for improvement. As you recall, level 1 gives feedback to the facilitator regarding style, implementation of instructional strategies, credibility, and so forth. Level 2 focuses in on content areas that the participants either learned or did not learn or whether or not they demonstrated a skill or demonstrated a behavior. If the participants are lacking in any of these areas, it could mean that the facilitator is not adequately covering the material or implementing the instructional strategies. Conversely, if the evaluation shows that participants are learning and adequately demonstrating the skill or behavior, it could mean that the facilitator is doing at least an adequate job.

Second, use level 2 evaluation for improving program design or content. The situation could mean that the course content or instructional strategies providing for learning and practice are lacking. If several participants are not doing well in a particular area, it could mean there is a course design/development problem often related to an issue with content or the instructional strategy. Conversely, if the participants are doing well, it likely means that there are no content or design/development issues.

Third, level 2 evaluation provides feedback to the participants on their learning. People like to know how they are doing. Level 2 can be used to provide a progress report to the participants. For example, one course designer who developed a client's account management program included tests and specific feedback on case presentations. This was a new approach for the audience. They loved it! One participant said, "It's great getting real feedback. Now I know if I am really learning anything." This feedback does not have to be general. By looking at specific questions or dimensions on the assessment instrument, the participant can zero in on the content area needing attention.

Fourth, using level 2 assessments can build credibility with your clients. In the case of the account management program described in the previous paragraph, the vice president of sales said that he was not sending another sales professional to any program and stopped all funding until the training organization could demonstrate that learning was taking place and that the course was making a difference. After the course designer explained the testing and the use of checklists that were built into the program, the vice president of sales was pleased. Participation and funding were restored.

Fifth, a pretest can be used for selecting the participants who need to attend the course or certain modules of the course. If you give a pretest and people score very high on all areas, do they need to take the course? Well, it depends. If the course is designed to shift only knowledge and not skill building, it is possible that the people do not need to attend. A course designed to teach Equal Employment Opportunity (EEO) laws or Occupational Safety and Health Act (OSHA) requirements may be designed to increase knowledge only. If so, people who already possess the knowledge would receive little direct benefit from taking the course. In other cases, a person already demonstrating some knowledge may be able to "place out of" some modules of a course. This is easier to do for an online or self-study course. If people are able to skip some modules because they already have the required knowledge, then you can save training expenses.

Last, you can link level 2 evaluation to other levels of evaluation. Again, take the opportunity to ask about extending the skills to the job and the impact they would have on the job and organization.

Level 2: What It Includes and Excludes

The evaluation of learning and practice is much more than just giving a pre- and posttest. It involves both knowledge and practices indicating that there has been a shift in the participants' capabilities in both areas. Table 5-1 summarizes what level 2 evaluation includes and excludes.

Advantages of Level 2 Evaluation

There are several advantages to conducting a level 2 evaluation. A major advantage is that level 2 evaluation reinforces the course content. Knowledge, skill, and behavioral assessments are developed directly from the course content. As participants take the assessments and receive feedback, the content and its application are revisited by

Table 5-1. Level 2: What's included and excluded?

Level 2 Evaluation Includes:	Level 2 Evaluation Excludes:
• Pretests (knowledge) • Interim tests (during the program) • Posttests (knowledge test given at the conclusion of the program) • Performance/application tests (usually assessments of the use of skills) • Observation of practice/application (use of checklists to evaluate for role plays, demonstrations, case studies, and so forth) • Work products (assessment of a deliverable that directly relates to the job)	• Reactions or perceptions of participants as captured in level 1 evaluation • Assessment of on-the-job performance, that is, actual behaviors and application on the job • Evaluation of environmental factors related to transfer • An assessment of the impact on the organization and ROI • Training costs • Evaluation of actual work products produced in the work environment

the participant. If the facilitator goes over the assessments, the participant gets another refresher. This should be part of the course design.

In addition, a pretest can even serve as a pre-course organizer for the participants, allowing them to think through some of the content before they take the course.

Assessments fulfill and are consistent with the learning objectives. For example, if there is a learning objective that the participants will be able to list the four levels of evaluation, there will be a test question asking them to list the four levels. If the participant is supposed to be able to recognize X, then there could be a matching or a multiple choice test to meet this objective.

Basic Rule 12
The course learning objectives dictate the type of assessment.

Level 2 evaluation holds the participant accountable for learning. Being present is not enough. Participants must now demonstrate the knowledge, skill, or behavior learned in the training. In some cases, there may be a standard imposed requiring that the participants achieve a certain score on the assessments in order to receive credit for the course. This approach adds some seriousness to the process. It becomes more important if the training is part of a certification effort. This approach supports the view that learners are accountable for their own learning and also links to the fourth advantage in that level 2 evaluation can hold the facilitator and course designers accountable. Course designers/developers must incorporate correct design principles, content, and instructional strategies to enhance learning. Facilitators must implement the design and engage the learners. If participants are not doing well on the assessments, the training organization must also look inward.

Think About This

Is it ever appropriate to use knowledge tests that are anonymous and used solely for the purpose of evaluating the effectiveness of the content or delivery? Yes, this could be done. If this practice is followed, you can still go over the test with the participants to provide them with feedback.

Disadvantages of Level 2 Evaluation

There are also some disadvantages to conducting level 2 evaluations. First, there still exists, even in adults, a fear of taking tests. Participants may also be concerned about how the results may be used. Be sure to tell the participants how the information will be used. Answer any questions regarding the use of test results. If you are using pre- and posttests to evaluate course design and delivery effectiveness, have the participants put a personal code on the pretest at the beginning of the course, and put the same code on the posttest at the end. That way, you can evaluate how individuals improved without knowing who they are.

Noted

Use the test results as feedback to participants and to reinforce content. This happens as they review their tests and you go over the test with them. If you must retain the tests, say, for item analysis, you still want to provide feedback to each participant on his or her performance on the test. You can accomplish this by providing a coversheet on the test for the participant's name and so forth. After the test has been scored, you can return the test to the appropriate participant for the review session based on the coversheet data. The participant can separate the coversheet from the test before it is returned to you, thereby ensuring the participant's anonymity.

Second, there could be legal issues regarding the use of the assessment results. In most cases, the tests have not been fully validated because of the high cost of doing so. If this is the case, use the results for developmental purposes only. Do not use the results for other HR-related decisions such as promotion, demotion, termination, pay increases, and so forth. Also, do not release individual information to your client. The participant is due privacy and anonymity. It is up to the participant to share his or her actual performance on any of the assessments.

Basic Rule 13
Only use test results for developmental purposes.

Next, knowledge and skill tests or behavioral assessments may not be good indicators of on-the-job use. Because an individual performs well in the learning environment does not mean he or she will perform well on the job. There are many environmental factors that influence the actual on-the-job use of the new knowledge, skills, and behaviors.

Last, not everyone performs well on tests or assessments. This may be a result of the fear factor or other individual issues. There could also be issues of the person not understanding the test questions due to limited reading ability.

Guidelines for Level 2 Evaluation

Consider this list of guidelines that can help you develop and implement level 2 evaluation:

▷ Complete the evaluation plan for levels 1 and 2. Remember, you must complete all previous levels of evaluation to support the current level of evaluation.

▷ The content covered in the level 2 assessment should directly relate to the course learning objectives.

▷ The content of the test questions or other assessments should come directly from the course content.

▷ The type of test (test format) or assessment must align with the course learning objectives.

Think About This

Always field test an assessment instrument with representatives of the target audience. This should be done during the course development stage and then again in the pilot. Then, conduct an item analysis following the testing to evaluate the questions by comparing the number of correct and incorrect answers for each item on the test. Also, be flexible to meet participant needs. For example, for someone who is vision-impaired or has limited literacy, it may be necessary to provide an oral test. You may also need to accommodate the needs of those for whom English is a second language. This could be done through translations or possibly by giving an oral test.

- ▷ Measure the learning of each participant. Sometimes executives or top performers believe that they are exceptional cases. This is not true. If they are in the target audience, they must fulfill all requirements. Even if an executive is just sitting in on a program, he or she needs to complete the assessment as a model to others.
- ▷ Use the pre- and posttest format to measure the shift in learning.
- ▷ If possible, compare the performance results for a control group (people who did not attend the training) to those of the experimental group (people who attended the training). This approach can be used to isolate the training content most relevant to the target audience.
- ▷ Use a variety of assessment methods, not just knowledge tests.
- ▷ Ensure that test items do not require the demonstration of knowledge or skills higher or lower than that taught in the course or required on the job.
- ▷ Conduct an item analysis to ensure that you have good test questions.
- ▷ Provide feedback to the participants as soon as possible.
- ▷ Use test results for developmental purposes only.

Developing Tests and Testing

The intent here is not to train you to write test questions. That is beyond the scope of this book. However, the content below will provide you with some guidelines and ideas that will be helpful as you begin developing tests. Table 5-2 summarizes some basic information about different types of tests.

Knowledge Tests

Creating knowledge tests requires a systematic process. Eliminating any of the steps may endanger the quality of the test and the value provided to the participants. Here are the basic steps:

1. Identify the course content areas for testing. These areas should link directly to the learning objectives and major concepts in the course.

2. Determine the test format (see table 5-2). Again, the type of test should align with the stated learning objectives as discussed above. A single test might include a true/false section, a multiple choice section, and an essay section, depending on the learning objectives and the type of test items they dictate.

3. Construct the test items. In constructing the test, determine the level of difficulty you want for a test question. Use Bloom's (1956) taxonomy to guide you in this area. Develop the stem, which concisely presents the problem, and then develop the options or choices for responding to the stem, including the correct answer and closely related distracters. Distracters are possible, but incorrect, answers. Generally, distracters can be determined wrong only by those who know the material. The correct answer must depend on the course content and not on someone's opinion or organizational practice.

Basic Rule 14
There should be only one correct answer.

4. Field test the learning assessment and revise it if needed. Take the test to a sample of the target audience and check for clarity, jargon, and any organizational red flags.

5. Conduct the test during the course pilot. This is your chance to try it out on the audience within the context of the training course.

6. Score the test.

7. Conduct an item analysis. Figure 5-1 is an example of an item analysis. To make decisions regarding facilitator skills, content, or instructional

Table 5-2. Choosing the most appropriate type of tests.

Type of Test	When to Use	Development Recommendations
True/False	• Is suitable when you want quick scoring • Requires little development time • Supports knowledge learning objectives that involve recall or recognition	• State questions in a clear and concise manner • Test one idea at a time • Provide one answer
Multiple Choice	• Allows you to assess learning objectively • Assesses learning of knowledge • Is appropriate when knowledge learning objective calls for recognizing	• Develop good distracters • Make all alternatives grammatically correct • Don't use a great deal of negatives • Provide four alternatives
Matching	• Is appropriate when learning objective calls for recognizing or identifying	• Provide 50% more options than the list of stem items • Keep all choices related • Keep the list of stem items to between five and 10
Listing	• Can be used when the learning objective calls for the participant to be able to list • Assesses recall • Is appropriate to use when the learning objective involves a set of steps that must go in a certain order	• Focus on one idea at a time • Keep the listings short (four to six items) • Keep each item short
Completion	• Is appropriate to use when the learning objective calls for the participant to be able to list items • Can be used to assess recall • Is appropriate to use when the desired answer is clear-cut and only a few word choices would be correct	• Do not copy the stem material directly from the participant material • Do not begin the question with a blank; keep them near the end • Avoid omitting more than one word • Provide options from the course material • Provide only one correct response, which should be from the participant material

(continued on page 80)

Table 5-2. Choosing the most appropriate type of tests (continued).

Type of Test	When to Use	Development Recommendations
Essay	• Is appropriate to use when you want to assess an entire concept • Can be good for objectives measuring attitudes, creativity, expression, and mental skill • Aligns with learning objectives asking the participant to explain or discuss	• Establish guidelines or criteria for evaluation of the essay in advance of reading the essays • Align the essay issue(s) with the course content • Provide enough time for the participant to complete the essay • Focus on specific issues presented in the training content • Use trained evaluators to score essays
Work Product Test	• Can be used when you want the participant to demonstrate a skill, a specific result, or follow a procedure • Aligns with learning objectives relating to developing, creating, making, designing, or demonstrating the steps in production	• Develop checklists, rating scales, or samples to judge the work product quality • Develop a behavioral observation checklist to assess whether participant followed the appropriate steps • May involve the judgment of an expert or panel of experts
Performance Test	• Assesses practice exercises or on-the-job application of the training content • Supports learning objectives indicating the participant will be able to apply or implement	• Develop a checklist or other instrument to consistently evaluate performance and/or behavior • Base the checklist on the course content • Determine a timeframe for taking the test • State the task or name the procedure to be performed • Provide any required tools, equipment, or aids to perform the test • Determine the scoring criteria and cutoff score if required • Provide instructions

strategies, you must analyze the results of participants' performance on assessments. An item analysis can indicate to the trainer areas where participants clearly understand and can apply the content. (They may have been able to do this prior to attending the class. If you didn't do a pretest, you really don't know.) The item analysis may also flag areas where a significant number of participants are not answering the question correctly (item 2 in figure 5-1, for example), possibly indicating that the facilitator was not adequately covering the material, the content was inaccurate or incomplete, the instructional strategies didn't allow for adequate practice, or the question was improperly constructed.

8. Revise the questions based on the item analysis.
9. Repeat the process until you finalize the assessment.

Assessments for Skills and Behaviors

You can also develop assessments to evaluate skills and behaviors. This is a type of performance demonstration. For example, assume you are training a person to be a facilitator (train-the-trainer or a separate session on facilitation skills). He or she is practicing facilitation skills as a concluding activity to the training workshop. You can assess skills by using a scaled checklist like the one in figure 5-2.

Or, let's say that you have just completed a course on selling skills and want to know if the participants can demonstrate certain behaviors. Figure 5-3 is a checklist that could be used to assess if the behaviors are being demonstrated. The checklist could be used in conjunction with a case study and role-play combination.

Self-Assessments

There is also the possibility of the participants doing self-assessments. Although self-assessments do not provide the same quality of information, they can serve as a pre-course module organizer and then as reinforcement. Figure 5-4 is a sample of this type of approach. Prior to the training, the participants review the content areas and self-rate each area according to a scale. Then, after the training, they reassess themselves, indicating their new level of knowledge and areas for further work. The example in figure 5-4 provides some sample content areas, but you could easily assess skills, specific knowledge areas, attitudes, or behaviors. As an evaluator, you could collect these forms and note the shift in the ratings.

Figure 5-1. Example of a partially completed item analysis.

The following matrix contains some results of a knowledge test composed of 20 items—15 multiple choice and five true/false. Six participants (1–6) took the assessment. The data is organized in a table for item analysis.

		Participants						Total Correct	Items Incorrect					
		1	2	3	4	5	6							
Item Number and Correct Answer									A	B	C	D	T	F
1	A	A	A	A	B	A	A	5	–	1	–	–		
2	B	B	B	C	C	C	C	2	–	–	4	–		
3	B	B	B	B	B	B	B	6	–	–	–	–		
4	D	D	D	D	C	D	D	5	–	–	1	–		
5	C	C	C	C	C	C	C	6	–	–	–	–		
6	B	B	B	A	B	C	D	3	1	–	1	1		
7	C	C	C	C	C	C	C	6	–	–	–	–		
8	A	A	A	A	A	A	C	5	–	–	1	–		
9	D	D	C	D	B	D	D	4	–	1	1	–		
10	D	D	D	D	D	D	D	6	–	–	–	–		
11	C	C	C	C	C	C	C							
12	A	C	A	A	C	A	C							
13	A	A	A	A	A	A	A							
14	C	C	C	C	D	C	C							
15	B	B	B	B	C	B	B							
16	T	T	T	T	T	T	T							
17	T	T	T	T	T	F	T							
18	F	F	F	F	F	F	F							
19	T	T	F	F	F	F	T							
20	F	F	F	F	F	F	F							
Total Correct Responses		19	18											

Figure 5-2. Example of a facilitation/presentation assessment.

Below is a list of behaviors describing the demonstration of facilitation/presentation skills. As an assessor, indicate the extent to which the individual demonstrates the listed behaviors. Use the following scale for your assessment.

1= to very little extent   2= to a moderate extent   3= to a great extent   4= to a very great extent

	1	2	3	4
Presentation/Facilitation Skills				
1. Uses appropriate verbal and nonverbal communication methodology				
2. Effectively uses voice (tone, projection, inflection), gestures, and eye contact				
3. Effectively uses examples, personal experiences, stories, and humor				
4. Effectively uses various questioning techniques				
5. Effectively paraphrases/restates participants' questions, comments, and observations				
6. Promotes participant discussion and involvement				
7. Manages group interaction, draws in quiet participants, and manages participants who try to monopolize the interaction				
Instructional/Learning Strategies				
8. Implements a variety of instructional/learning strategies (such as guided discussions, case studies, role plays, small group work with feedback, assessments)				
9. Facilitates debriefs so all learning is processed				
10. Effectively applies a variety of media (video, overheads, computer projection, wallboards, props, flipcharts) effectively				
11. Models participant-centered and not leader-centered behavior				

Reprinted with permission from Performance Advantage Group, 2004.

Figure 5-3. Example of a selling process behavioral checklist.

This is a behavioral/demonstration checklist for selling skills. It could be used to determine if the learner is demonstrating the correct behaviors as demonstrated in a role play. The role play would need to be in the context of a case study or possibly a job simulation.

The yes/no format indicates only if the behavior was exhibited and, therefore, does not connote quality.

Preparation	Yes	No
Develops specific objectives for the call that define the expected results		
Acquires up-to-date information about the customer through all available resources		
Develops action plans that anticipate questions and objections		
Opening		
Establishes rapport with the customer by discussing areas of interest		
Reduces barriers to effective communications		
Uses a sales attention-getter		
Creating Interest		
Sets an agenda by stating the purpose and objectives		
Gains agreement on expectations for the call		
Uses an initial benefit statement to create interest		
Identifying/Confirming Needs		
Engages the customer through active listening and asking open-ended questions		
Asks specific questions about the customer's specific needs		
Explores options and gains agreement on alternatives		
Recommendations		
Uses features, advantages, and benefits to present recommendations		
Recognizes buying signals and uses a trial close technique		
Summarizes important benefits and then asks for a commitment		
Handles customer objections		
Develops a plan of action		
Follow-up		
Reviews outcome of the call		
Maintains customer relationship		
Keeps customer updated		

Reprinted with permission from Performance Advantage Group, 2004.

Figure 5-4. Example of a self-assessment instrument.

Staffing Plans

The purpose of the pre/post self-assessment is to provide you with an opportunity to identify areas where you are confident in your knowledge about staffing plans and areas where you may need to do some additional study or receive additional training.

First, go through the pretraining assessment and circle your perceived level of knowledge for each area designated. Then, where you are not satisfied with your current knowledge level, focus on those areas in the course.

After your training, conduct the posttraining assessment. Review each area and note the shift in your ratings. Place a checkmark by the content areas you want to review.

Use the following scale to indicate your level of knowledge in the areas described:

1 = Poor or low   2 = Moderate or good   3 = High or excellent

	Pretraining Assessment			Posttraining Assessment			Review (✓)
Implement Staffing Plans							
Factors or components of an annual (short-term) staffing plan	1	2	3	1	2	3	
Considerations for agent staffing plan	1	2	3	1	2	3	
Models for staffing plan (forecasting)	1	2	3	1	2	3	
Forecasting agents	1	2	3	1	2	3	
Matching workforce composition to cost, structure, competition, and labor supply	1	2	3	1	2	3	
Methods of forecasting	1	2	3	1	2	3	
Special considerations for seven-day/24-hour operations (24/7)	1	2	3	1	2	3	
The workforce mix, including advantages and disadvantages	1	2	3	1	2	3	
Factors to determine the appropriate mix	1	2	3	1	2	3	
Work schedules: flex-time, compressed work week, remote or telecommute	1	2	3	1	2	3	
Benefits and issues of a remote staff	1	2	3	1	2	3	
Tactics to address the issues	1	2	3	1	2	3	

Reprinted with permission from Performance Advantage Group, 2004.

Think About This

For behavioral or performance assessment, you need to specify the elements to be measured and determine how closely the performance models the training. Remember, the training should closely replicate reality.

Testing: What to Do and What Not to Do

Table 5-3 summarizes the do's and don'ts of testing. Although this is by no means a complete listing, it does capture some of the more important aspects of testing.

Benefits of Testing

Developing tests is a complex and time-consuming process. It takes specific expertise to develop good assessments to measure learning. Therefore, there must be significant benefits to warrant this effort. Some of the benefits of testing include:

- ▶ Testing identifies content areas that have been learned or where more reinforcement is needed to support learning.
- ▶ Testing highlights the areas of training that are retained.
- ▶ Knowledge tests and assessments can measure individual change and assess individual abilities.
- ▶ It is one way to evaluate training effectiveness.
- ▶ Assessments reinforce what was learned.
- ▶ Pretests can be an advance organizer for the program.
- ▶ Tests can gauge the knowledge level of the group.
- ▶ Assessments can be used to assess how well the facilitator is presenting the material.

Why Participants Resist Testing

With all these benefits, you would think that participants would embrace testing. Yet, this is not the case. In many instances, participants resist testing. One reason is that they fear they may be embarrassed by the test results. Results should be kept confidential, but many times tests are scored and handed back during the training. Others may see the results of their peers. A poor performance can be embarrassing. Likewise, sometimes good results can result in embarrassment if top performers get teased about their high scores.

Table 5-3. The do's and don'ts of testing.

What to Do	What Not To Do
• Do develop enough test questions to sample the material and provide for reliability.	• Don't rely on a single type of test question. For example, do not make a test up of all true and false or all multiple choice questions.
• Do align the type of test question with the learning objective.	• Don't assume that all participants understand the test format.
• Do weight all test items the same. For example, don't have multiple choice questions worth 2 points each and true/false questions worth 1 point each.	• Don't copy material directly from the participant manual for testing.
• Do write test questions based on what you want the participants to know. Base the test on the more important aspects of the course content.	• Don't provide an answer that would be obvious even to those not knowing the material.
• Do test for the ability of the participants to apply the skills and concepts in the course.	• Don't make the question so complex that the learner cannot understand what is being asked.
• Do develop good distracters to determine if the participants really know and understand the course content.	• Don't make the stem so general that the learner does not know what is being asked.
• Do provide clear and complete instructions.	• Don't write the stem and options such that they are not grammatically correct.
• Do provide an example of the type of test question.	
• Do test only one idea in each question.	
• Do provide only one possible answer to the test question.	
• Do vary the response pattern.	

Second, sometimes there is the fear of how the information will be used. Participants still fear that their performance on assessments will affect merit raises or opportunities for promotion.

Third, tests can pinpoint areas of weakness. With this knowledge comes the responsibility to improve. This could then result in additional work.

Types of Level 2 Assessments and Their Advantages and Disadvantages

Several types of assessments can provide insights into whether the participant is learning and can apply the new knowledge, skills, or behavior. Table 5-4 summarizes these assessments.

Table 5-4. A closer look at assessment methods.

Assessment Type	Advantages	Disadvantages
Written Tests (Includes Pre- and Posttests)	• Can provide immediate feedback • Easy to administer • Flexible in timing • Reinforces content • Can be a pre-course organizer • Provides documentation • Can be an instructional strategy	• Can create anxiety and stress • Is difficult to construct • Has some legal implications
Performance Tests and Assessments	• Provides for application of the content • Encourages management attention • Can be an instructional strategy • Reinforces content • Simulates the job • Can provide immediate feedback • Can be used to assess procedures	• May require a relatively significant amount of time • Has some legal implications • Must have trained observers with checklists • Cannot identify factors other than training that may affect performance
Skill Test	• Allows for application • Can be an instructional strategy • Can reinforce a corporate performance standard • Replicates the job • Supports job standards • Reinforces skills	• Must have trained observers • Requires a checklist (yes/no or scaled) • May be difficult to determine the level of performance • Has some legal implications
Work Product	• Allows for application • Supports job standards • Can be an instructional strategy • Reinforces the use of a procedure • Simulates the job • Can be used on the job, supporting transfer • Can involve subject matter experts • Provides for high visibility • Can assess skills and the supporting procedure	• Must have knowledgeable and skilled evaluators • Is time consuming • May be limited to the availability of equipment • Could disrupt the work environment • Has some legal implications • May be difficult to construct • Involves greater risks because of its high visibility

Think About This

If the participants can demonstrate that they can apply the knowledge, skills, or behavior in the course through some practice and assessment, there is a greater probability that they can apply it on the job. In addition, if you can demonstrate the application of the knowledge, skill, or behavior in the training, you have a strong link to support positive level 3 evaluation results.

Getting It Done

This chapter introduced you to the basics of level 2 evaluation for assessing the extent to which participants learned new knowledge, skills, abilities, and behaviors and how well they are able to demonstrate their new learning within the context of the training session.

Often level 2 evaluation involves testing or other assessments of learning. Exercise 5-1 offers you the opportunity to try an item analysis, which can point out problems with the training or with the test itself by highlighting items that were problematic for the participants.

To see how well you did with the item analysis, compare your answers to the completed item analysis on page 92.

Next, to demonstrate your understanding of level 2, complete the evaluation plan through level 2 for one of your courses (exercise 5-2).

Now that you have an understanding of level 1 (reaction) and level 2 (evaluation for knowledge; demonstration of skills and behaviors), you are ready to embark on level 3 to evaluate the amount of transfer that has taken place and the work environment.

Exercise 5-1. Doing an item analysis.

The exercise below should look familiar because it was presented earlier in the chapter to demonstrate how an item analysis is performed (figure 5-1). Please complete the item analysis for a knowledge test composed of 20 questions—15 multiple choice and five true/false. Six participants took the assessment. You are to:

1. Complete the results chart.
2. Identify potential issues and possible causes.
3. Determine which participants would pass the learning assessment if the criterion reference passing score were 85 percent.
4. Determine how well the class as a whole performed on the assessment.

	Participants						Total Correct	Items Incorrect					
	1	2	3	4	5	6							
Item Number and Correct Answer								A	B	C	D	T	F
1 A	A	A	A	B	A	A	5	–	1	–	–		
2 B	B	B	C	C	C	C	2	–	–	4	–		
3 B	B	B	B	B	B	B	6	–	–	–	–		
4 D	D	D	D	C	D	D	5	–	–	1	–		
5 C	C	C	C	C	C	C	6	–	–	–	–		
6 B	B	B	A	B	C	D	3	1	–	1	1		
7 C	C	C	C	C	C	C	6	–	–	–	–		
8 A	A	A	A	A	A	C	5	–	–	1	–		
9 D	D	C	D	B	D	D	4	–	1	1	–		
10 D	D	D	D	D	D	D	6	–	–	–	–		
11 C	C	C	C	C	C	C							
12 A	C	A	A	C	A	C							
13 A	A	A	A	A	A	A							
14 C	C	C	C	D	C	C							
15 B	B	B	B	C	B	B							
16 T	T	T	T	T	T	T							
17 T	T	T	T	T	F	T							
18 F	F	F	F	F	F	F							
19 T	T	F	F	F	F	T							
20 F	F	F	F	F	F	F							
Total Correct Responses	19	18											

Exercise 5-2. Complete a level 1 and level 2 evaluation plan.

Evaluation Plan: Level 1 (Reaction) and Level 2 (Learning and Application)

Business Metric(s): _____

	What	Why	How	Sources	When	Where	Who
Level 1 Reaction							
Level 2 Learning							
Level 2 Application							

Solution to exercise 5-1.

1. Complete the results chart. *See the completed chart below.*
2. Identify potential issues and possible causes. *Items 2, 12, and 19: Possible reasons why many participants arrived at the wrong answer could be (1) the item is confusing, or (2) the content was not covered adequately during the training.*
3. Determine which participants would pass the learning assessment if the criterion reference passing score were 85 percent. *A score of 17 or better would be required to pass. Therefore, participants 1, 2, and 3 would pass.*
4. Determine how well the class as a whole performed on the assessment. *The class as a whole scored 98 correct responses out of a possible 120 (81.67 percent).*

	Participants							Items Incorrect					
	1	**2**	**3**	**4**	**5**	**6**	**Total Correct**						
Item Number and Correct Answer								A	B	C	D	T	F
1 A	A	A	A	B	A	A	5	–	1	–	–		
2 B	B	B	C	C	C	C	2	–	–	4	–		
3 B	B	B	B	B	B	B	6	–	–	–	–		
4 D	D	D	D	C	D	D	5	–	–	1	–		
5 C	C	C	C	C	C	C	6	–	–	–	–		
6 B	B	B	A	B	C	D	3	1	–	1	1		
7 C	C	C	C	C	C	C	6	–	–	–	–		
8 A	A	A	A	A	A	C	5	–	–	1	–		
9 D	D	C	D	B	D	D	4	–	1	1	–		
10 D	D	D	D	D	D	D	6	–	–	–	–		
11 C	C	C	C	C	C	C	6	–	–	–	–		
12 A	C	A	A	C	A	C	3	–	–	3	–		
13 A	A	A	A	A	A	A	6	–	–	–	–		
14 C	C	C	C	D	C	C	5	–	–	–	1		
15 B	B	B	B	C	B	B	5	–	–	1	–		
16 T	T	T	T	T	T	T	6					–	–
17 T	T	T	T	T	F	T	5					–	1
18 F	F	F	F	F	F	F	6					–	–
19 T	T	F	F	F	F	T	2					–	4
20 F	F	F	F	F	F	F	6					–	–
Total Correct Responses	19	18	17	12	16	16	98/120 81.67%						

6

Level 3:
Transfer to the Job
and the Environment

▪ ▪

What's Inside This Chapter

In this chapter, you'll learn:

▶ A working definition of transfer
▶ Business case for transfer
▶ What level 3 evaluation includes and what it excludes
▶ Requirements for transfer
▶ Guidelines for transfer
▶ Barriers to transfer
▶ Evaluation of the design to ensure transfer
▶ Instruments to support and assess transfer.

A Working Definition of Transfer

The basic idea of transfer is simple. Transfer is taking something from one place to another. When you transfer funds, you move them from one account to another. Likewise, when you transfer training, you are moving the acquisition of the knowledge, skills, and abilities from the learning environment to the job. The result is that what was learned in one situation is now being applied in another situation.

According to Broad and Newstrom (1992), "Transfer of training is the effective and continuing application, by trainees to their jobs, of the knowledge and skills

93

gained in training—both on and off the job." Notice use of the word "continuing." This is an important concept. If a learner returns to work and begins to use the learned skills but then stops using them as job demands begin to take hold or when the manager fails to provide needed support, then transfer did not take place.

The Business Case for Transfer

There is a business case for making transfer a top priority in the design of a learning experience. First, organizations spend billions of dollars each year on training. When you consider the direct costs, time off the job, and opportunity cost, companies make a substantial investment in training. Given this investment, managers want some assurances that the training and subsequent improvements in employee performance will be used to help them meet business objectives.

Second, much of the training that is currently implemented is not used on the job; transfer does not take place as it should. According to Broad and Newstrom (1992), ". . . most of that investment in organizational training and development is wasted because most of the knowledge and skills gained in training (well over 80 percent, by some estimates) is not fully applied by those employees on the job." Some reasons for the failure to transfer relate to program design and development, lack of immediate supervisory support, and an unsupportive organizational culture.

Third, high-quality HRD, which adds value through transfer, is important for recruitment and retention. Potential job candidates and new recruits expect development plans that provide value not only to their own job performance and to the organization, but also to them personally. Knowledge, skills, and abilities that do not transfer cannot help them advance their careers.

Fourth, given the state of business competition, improving the capabilities of the workforce is critical. Because the only sustainable competitive advantage is the intellect of the organization, the training organization plays a critical role in developing and ensuring the use of the knowledge, skills, and abilities required for current and future success.

What Transfer Evaluation Includes and Excludes

The evaluation of transfer is much more than just seeing if some of the training is used on the job. It involves not just the use, but also the new knowledge, skills, and abilities consistently used on the job; how much of the content transferred to the job, and the environmental factors that support or hinder the transfer process. Table 6-1 summarizes what level 3 evaluation includes and excludes.

Table 6-1. Level 3: What's included and excluded?

Level 3 Evaluation Includes:	Level 3 Evaluation Excludes:
• Pre- and posttraining instrument comparisons, as with performance contracts • On-the-job performance measures compared to pretraining baseline • Observation of application on the job • Interviews with managers, peers, and possibly customers • Assessment of the environment • Use of performance contracts, action plans, learning contracts, and so forth • Focus groups • Performance/application tests on the job	• Reaction evaluation or perceptions • Testing for learning • Performance/application tests during the training • Classroom assessments • Organizational results or impact • Monetary value of the change (benefit) • ROI • Training costs

Requirements for Transfer

There are several conditions that must be present for transfer to take place. Some of these relate to the participant, others to management, and still others to the corporate environment. For transfer to take place, the requirements include the following:

1. The learner must be motivated to improve his or her performance. If there is not a perceived need, it will be difficult for learning and transfer to take place.

Think About This

If attendance is mandatory, participants might be occupying the classroom seats, but that does not mean that learning takes place. Participation does not equate to learning.

2. The learner must recognize both the need and the area to be improved. That's why needs assessment is important. Needs assessment identifies the performance requirements and the gaps between current performance and the desired performance. Then, needs assessment identifies the knowledge, skills, and abilities necessary to close the gap. All this information is provided by

the needs assessment. This is also why management coaching and feedback is important. Through coaching, the employee becomes aware of the gap in performance and his or her knowledge, skills, and abilities. The coach also provides feedback on performance as it relates to the closing of the performance gap.

Noted

It is not enough for a manager to send an employee to training; the manager must be involved in the learning to a greater extent. The manager must provide direct feedback to the person regarding the area of performance deficiency and explain how the training can help to close the performance gap. The consequences of closing the performance gap or failing to do so must also be discussed. This frank discussion helps to motivate the person and identifies the direct need and area for improvement. Does all training need to be directed toward overcoming a weakness? Not necessarily. Sometimes training is used to help learners hone a skill that is already a strength. If excellence of performance comes from using strengths, a discussion could take place to identify an area of strength and look at ways to make it even better.

3. The work and organization environment must support the use of the new knowledge, skills, or abilities on the job. The manager needs to provide coaching to help the trainee apply what was learned, and the manager needs to provide the resources necessary for application on the job. Too often, a learner returns to the job only to find a supervisor who wants things done the same old way. The learner may need help in fulfilling the performance contract or implementing the action plans. Peer support also

Think About This

Recognition can also be provided by way of assignments. For example, after a learner returns to the job, the manager indicates that as a result of the performance improvement that the learner will receive a good, challenging assignment that will provide exposure to key individuals.

helps transfer happen. Additionally, the recognition and reward system needs to support the transfer process. Such rewards can range from verbal acknowledgment, to the opportunity to train other staff members, to financial incentives.

4. To support transfer, the learners must receive the help necessary to apply the new knowledge, skills, or abilities. In some cases, this could be some additional on-the-job training as follow-up. It could mean that a top performer provides coaching. In other cases, it could be as simple as providing the person with the appropriate information or tools and equipment.

5. Management must support the transfer by providing the opportunity to use the new knowledge, skills, or abilities. Without use, the learning will fade. Both the manager and learner should expect immediate application to the job.

Noted

Timing is an issue in transfer. Sometimes training is provided well in advance of when the trainee will actually use the new knowledge, skills, or abilities. For example, the organization is getting new equipment that persons must be trained on. A training session is provided using the vendor's equipment. The actual equipment is installed four months later. There is little probability that the learner will actually remember how to use the equipment.

6. Provide for posttraining reinforcement, goal setting, coaching, and feedback. The learner may need a refresher, job aid, or some mechanism for continued reinforcement of the new knowledge, skills, or abilities. This is a design issue. In addition, through such strategies as performance contracts, learning contracts, and action planning, the learner can make plans in conjunction with his or her manager to transfer the learning to the job. Coaching and feedback are necessary to reinforce proper use and to correct any inappropriate application of the learning.

Basic Rule 15
Provide the training near the time the learning will be needed on the job.

Guidelines for Transfer

Having a learning experience that considers transfer in the design process is critical to successful application. You can hardly expect a learner to use the skills if there has not been an opportunity for practice, if there are no strategies to support transfer, or if the environment was not prepared.

Given these requirements, there are guidelines for conducting a level 3 evaluation. First, allow enough time for the change to take place. The individual must have the opportunity to implement the new knowledge, skills, or abilities and for the environment to take its effect. For example, if you are teaching supervisors to conduct an effective feedback session during a performance appraisal, then the supervisors must wait until they can conduct a performance appraisal. If, however, you are teaching time management, these skills can be implemented immediately. Generally, you need to wait three to six months before conducting level 3 evaluation to see if transfer has occurred.

Second, conduct a pre- and posttraining analysis. Before the training, evaluate the knowledge, skills, and ability level of the learner. This is the baseline data. Then, at a later date (according to the evaluation plan), measure again the knowledge, skill, and ability level on the job. By making the before-and-after comparison, you can determine if there was a change and the magnitude of that change.

Third, you can use an interview or survey to determine if there has been a perceived change in performance attributable to the acquisition of new knowledge, skills, or abilities. Again, this is part of the evaluation plan. You need to determine whom to interview or survey. You could get information from the learners, their supervisor or peers, or possibly subordinates. The idea is to use the sources that can provide the most accurate and timely information.

Fourth, be sure the learning experience is designed for transfer. The needs assessment must identify the needs related to the learners, the learning objectives must indicate the use on the job, the content should directly support the needs assessment and job requirements, and the instructional strategies should provide a structure to support transfer.

Next, determine the costs related to the evaluation effort. The costs should then be weighed against the expected benefits from the evaluation. When considering costs, include all costs, such as time of staff to develop, implement, and analyze the instruments and results; the time of persons supplying the information; distribution costs; any costs associated with outside support as a consultant; and so forth. The benefits here are the benefits of conducting the evaluation, not the benefits of the training. (That is the goal of level 4 evaluation.) The value of the evaluation is based on the what and why of the evaluation plan. Because training is very expensive, knowing the extent of use and the environmental factors supporting or hindering transfer can save the organization a great deal of money.

Think About This

Transfer must take place for the training to have an impact and ROI. Level 3 evaluation establishes the link between use on the job and impact. Therefore, you must demonstrate that the new knowledge, skills, and abilities are being used on the job in order to justify any impact and ROI that is due to the training.

Last, involve the client in the planning and data collection. Remember, evaluation is used to make decisions. These decisions are determined during the development of the evaluation plan. The extent of the evaluation and analysis is bound by the decisions to be made. So, involve the client in the evaluation planning process for level 3, communicate with him or her about the results, and make some joint decisions regarding next steps.

Basic Rule 16

Do not do more evaluation and analysis than is required to support the decisions identified in the evaluation plan.

Barriers to Transfer

Broad and Newstrom (1992) conducted a couple of studies to identify trainers' perceptions about barriers to transfer. In order of their perceived importance, the barriers are the following:

1. lack of reinforcement on the job
2. interference from immediate (work) environment

3. unsupportive organizational culture
4. learners' perception of impractical training programs
5. learners' perception of irrelevant training content
6. learners' discomfort with change and associated effort
7. separation from inspiration or support of the trainer
8. learners' perception of poorly designed/delivered training
9. pressure from peers to resist change.

Broad and Newstrom's barriers to transfer can then be classified as affecting training before, during, or after training. Although these barriers make sense, realize that they are from a trainer's perspective, not from the view of participants or management. Nevertheless, it is possible to make some generalizations regarding these barriers to transfer:

1. Lack of reinforcement on the job is a huge barrier to transfer.
2. Another major factor inhibiting transfer is the lack of support by the immediate environment (work and time pressures, insufficient authority, ineffective work process, inadequate equipment or facilities, lack of opportunity to use skills, and inadequate instructions on the job to perform the skills differently).
3. Most barriers to transfer occur after training.
4. Managers are instrumental to resolving the problem of transfer.
5. Trainers are responsible for problems concerning content, design, and facilitation.

Evaluation of the Design to Ensure Transfer

The strategies to solve the transfer problem are not the focus of this book, but evaluation is. Therefore, you can evaluate the quality or completeness of the training process to facilitate the transfer process. The instrument presented in figure 6-1 provides a way to conduct such an evaluation. The instrument looks at what can be done before, during, and after the training by HRD staff, the participant, peers of the participant, and the manager. Of course, you will want to add some of your own factors and delete those that do not apply to your situation.

Basic Rule 17

When evaluating the course design for transfer, include the HRD staff, the participants, and participants' managers and peers.

Figure 6-1. An instrument for evaluating a program's potential for transfer.

Using a scale from 0 to 5, indicate the extent to which the dimension was implemented before, during, or after the training program:

0 = not at all   1 = to a very little extent   2 = to a little extent
3 = to some extent   4 = to a great extent   5 = to a very great extent

BEFORE TRAINING

Manager's Actions						
Provided input into the needs analysis	0	1	2	3	4	5
Reviewed program content and instructional strategies during the design/development phase for job application	0	1	2	3	4	5
Selected those to be trained based on some established criteria	0	1	2	3	4	5
Attended the training prior to their reports taking the training	0	1	2	3	4	5
Collected baseline data to measure performance change	0	1	2	3	4	5
Established performance goals based on the training	0	1	2	3	4	5
Met with the participant prior to the training to discuss • the importance of the training for the participant • program content and objectives • expectations for use on the job • expected impact for the organization	0	1	2	3	4	5
Set up a meeting between the participant(s) and others who have gone through the program to help prepare the participant	0	1	2	3	4	5
Grouped peers (co-workers) or team members so they could attend together	0	1	2	3	4	5
Mutually developed a performance or learning contract	0	1	2	3	4	5
Identified barriers to transfer	0	1	2	3	4	5

(continued on page 102)

Figure 6-1. An instrument for evaluating a program's potential for transfer (continued).

Participant's Actions						
Provided input into the needs assessment	0	1	2	3	4	5
Provided input into the course content and instructional strategies for job application	0	1	2	3	4	5
Completed the performance contract or learning contact with the manager	0	1	2	3	4	5
Asked and got answers to the following questions: • Why was I elected to go? • Is it relevant to my current or future job? How much of it is relevant to my job? • What opportunities will I have to apply the content? • What support will I receive upon return to the job? • Am I prepared? Do I need background information?	0	1	2	3	4	5
Completed the course pre-work	0	1	2	3	4	5
Identified potential barriers to transfer	0	1	2	3	4	5
HRD Professionals' Actions						
Conducted needs assessment on which program content is based	0	1	2	3	4	5
Wrote learning objectives for application to the job	0	1	2	3	4	5
Developed program content that aligns with the organization's business plan	0	1	2	3	4	5
Involved managers and participants in the design and development process	0	1	2	3	4	5
Designed instructional strategies for practice and application	0	1	2	3	4	5
Peers' Actions						
Told future participants of the program content	0	1	2	3	4	5
Told future participants how they are using the new knowledge, skills, and abilities	0	1	2	3	4	5
Provided supportive comments around the program content and facilitator	0	1	2	3	4	5
Shared any course materials from when they attended	0	1	2	3	4	5
Offered to cover the workload while others are in training	0	1	2	3	4	5

DURING TRAINING

Manager's Actions						
Participated in the training, in such ways as • made presentations • reviewed work products • evaluated learning activities • assisted in recognition efforts	0	1	2	3	4	5
Protected participant's time; did not allow interruptions	0	1	2	3	4	5
Delegated participant's workload to others	0	1	2	3	4	5
Assisted in developing participant's action plans	0	1	2	3	4	5
Participant's Actions						
Participated actively in the program	0	1	2	3	4	5
Established a support group that extended into the field	0	1	2	3	4	5
Maintained an "Applying the Concepts" log to quickly record possible applications of content	0	1	2	3	4	5
Developed the performance contract, learning contract, and/or action plans	0	1	2	3	4	5
Wrote the letter to the manager	0	1	2	3	4	5
Developed strategies to address barriers to transfer	0	1	2	3	4	5
HRD Professionals' Actions						
Managed the learning process, that is, implemented the instructional strategies and assessments	0	1	2	3	4	5
Provided individual and group feedback	0	1	2	3	4	5
Simulated the actual work of the job	0	1	2	3	4	5
Provided opportunity for participants to develop support groups	0	1	2	3	4	5
Held participants accountable for development of performance contract, learning contract, action plans, and so forth	0	1	2	3	4	5
Provided recognition	0	1	2	3	4	5
Peers' Actions						
Covered the workload	0	1	2	3	4	5
Did not interrupt the sessions	0	1	2	3	4	5

(continued on page 104)

Figure 6-1. An instrument for evaluating a program's potential for transfer (continued).

AFTER TRAINING

Manager's Actions						
Planned for the transition back to the job with follow-up discussions on the application of training content	0	1	2	3	4	5
Provided opportunities to use the new knowledge, skills, or abilities	0	1	2	3	4	5
Provided coaching and feedback for reinforcement	0	1	2	3	4	5
Provided recognition	0	1	2	3	4	5
Provided resources for implementation of the performance contract, learning contract, or action plans	0	1	2	3	4	5
Required the participant to peer-teach content to staff	0	1	2	3	4	5
Reduced work demands while participants gain proficiency	0	1	2	3	4	5
Provided (and expected) the use of job aids	0	1	2	3	4	5
Allowed refresher training	0	1	2	3	4	5
Removed barriers to transfer	0	1	2	3	4	5
Participant's Actions						
Reviewed program content	0	1	2	3	4	5
Implemented performance contract, learning contract, or action plans	0	1	2	3	4	5
Secured a mentor	0	1	2	3	4	5
Secured peer coaching	0	1	2	3	4	5
Maintained participation in the support group	0	1	2	3	4	5
Applied the new knowledge, skills, and abilities to the job	0	1	2	3	4	5
Implemented strategies to address barriers to transfer	0	1	2	3	4	5
HRD Professionals' Actions						
Conducted level 3 evaluation	0	1	2	3	4	5
Followed up with such questions as:	0	1	2	3	4	5
• How are you able to use the skills on the job?						
• What kind of support are you receiving?						
• Which program concepts, content have you used?						
• What hinders you from using the skills?						

Implement such follow-up actions as: • Follow-up sessions (for example, classroom, intranet) • Continued readings	0	1	2	3	4	5
Developed intranet support through bulletin board, chat, and so forth for coaching and peer support	0	1	2	3	4	5
Peers' Actions						
Supported—verbally and by actions—the use of the new knowledge, skills, and abilities	0	1	2	3	4	5
Became part of the ongoing support group (if previously attended the training)	0	1	2	3	4	5
Provided peer coaching	0	1	2	3	4	5

Reprinted with permission from Performance Advantage Group, 2004.

Think About This

Before deploying an instrument or method for level 3 evaluation, you should ask some questions about

- how the instrument or method will be implemented and when
- how the use of job aids or other materials can support and reinforce the training
- the use of specific skills on the job, including frequency and proficiency
- the importance and relevance of training content
- relevance of content for the learners' peers
- the change in performance resulting from the training.

Instruments and Methods to Support and Assess Transfer

Several instruments and methods can support transfer and also serve as mechanisms to assess the extent to which transfer took place. You also need to assess the environment to identify the barriers and enablers that hinder or support transfer. As part of the course design, some instruments must be developed and incorporated to support transfer.

The Performance Contract

The performance contract helps prepare the participant for the program and helps ensure that the content will transfer to the job. The purposes of the performance contract are to

▶ provide a format for the participant and manager to jointly identify and discuss how the course content will be used on the job
▶ identify resources and support necessary for successful transfer of the learning
▶ identify any barriers and their solution to successful transfer of the learning
▶ secure joint agreement of these initial plans.

The performance contract is for planning purposes and is meant to be modified during and immediately after the training program. It also serves as a pre-course organizer. Through advance planning, the participant can focus on course content directly relevant to his or her needs. In addition, the joint meeting can result in the manager's involvement in the participant's continued learning through on-the-job use of the new knowledge, skills, and abilities. Figure 6-2 provides an example of a performance contract.

Figure 6-2. Example of a performance contract.

Purpose: Briefly describe your purpose for taking this course

1. We need to reduce our turnover. I am looking for ways to reduce turnover or increase retention.
2. Diversity is becoming a big issue for us. I need to recruit and then better utilize a diverse workforce.
3. I want to become certified and add this as a credential.

On-the-Job Requirements: Indicate your specific job assignment(s). This could also be a performance or professional development objective that necessitates the use of content/concepts from this course. Identify those concepts or content areas and indicate initial actions you will take to implement those concepts.

Job Assignment/Objective	Related Course Concepts (Write in the Course Sections That Apply)	Implementation Actions
Objective A. To develop and implement retention strategies resulting in a 5% reduction in our turnover over the next two years.	• Section 2 on identifying causes and costs of turnover. • Section 2 on factors affecting retention and strategies for retention.	• Identify causal factors. • Identify and implement strategies or actions to reduce turnover or increase retention.

Job Assignment/Objective	Related Course Concepts (Write in the Course Sections That Apply)	Implementation Actions
Objective B. To recruit and better utilize a diverse workforce.	• Section 3 on recruiting a diverse workforce and on methods and sources for recruiting. • Section 8 on implications of diversity and diversity programs.	• (To be determined from the course.)
Objective C. Improve my knowledge and skills in call center people management through training and CIAC certification.	• All sections of the course.	• Attend course. • Complete the "learning tests" during the course and identify areas for additional self-learning. • Implement the performance contract items with my manager. • Take and pass the CIAC assessment.

Barriers: Identify potential significant problems/barriers to implementing your performance contract and possible solutions to those problems/barriers.

Problems/Barriers	Solutions
Objective A. • Identification of the root causes. • Management support.	• Development of a complete plan and solicit support from the required groups. • Others to be determined in the program.
Objective B. • Acceptance of diversity within the organization. • Resources for additional recruiting.	• Build the business case. • Diversity training. • Link with HR and secure resources.
Objective C. • Time to complete the training and study required for success. • Budget to the additional CIAC training courses.	• Incorporate the CIAC training into my development and career plans. • Get approval from upper management for my personal development approach.

(continued on page 108)

Figure 6-2. Example of a performance contract (continued).

Resources/Support Requirements and Enablers: Indicate the resources and/or management support required to implement your performance contract. Identify the factors, processes, or people that provide required support to implementing your performance contract and indicate the support needed (enablers).

Resources, Support, and Enablers	Specifics of the Requirement
Objective A. • Support of other groups that might be involved. • Budget to implement strategies.	• To be determined during the course.
Objective B. • HR support to locate recruiting sources and development of materials. • Budget for recruiting. • Management and employee support for acceptance of diversity.	• Development of recruiting materials directed at a diverse audience. • (To be determined during the course.)
Objective C. • My manager's approval to pursue the complete CIAC certification learning program. • Budget and time to support the development. • Support from staff.	• Attend all four CIAC course training sessions and pass CIAC knowledge and skill assessments. • Complete the CIAC "360 Review." • Complete The CIAC "Work Product."

_____   _____

Participant's Signature   Date   Manager's Signature   Date

Reprinted with permission from Performance Advantage Group, 2004.

Think About This

For the performance contract to be of greatest benefit, the participant and manager must understand the course objectives and content. This means that the training organization needs to fully communicate to participants and their managers the necessary information to support the performance contract.

After the program, you can evaluate the extent to which the performance contract has been fulfilled. This evaluation may include specific questions related to the use of the course content and the support provided to remove barriers and enhance enablers to transfer.

Applying-the-Concepts Form

Another instrument to support transfer is the applying-the-concepts form. Many times, as the content is being presented, the lights come on for a participant and he or she gets an inspiration about how to use the concept. The problem is that there is no structured way to capture the idea. An applying-the-concepts form provides that structure (figure 6-3). This form can easily be provided as a handout or embedded in the introduction to the participant manual. Then, after the course, you can contact the participants and see the extent to which they have implemented their ideas from their applying-the-concepts form.

Figure 6-3. An example of an applying-the-concepts form.

The first row in this template has been completed for you as an example. Add rows as necessary to customize the form for your course.

Concept/Idea/Principle	Application to My Job	Resources/Support Needed
Develop an evaluation plan	• More complete evaluation of training courses (specific courses to be determined) • Can demonstrate value • Engage the client • Improve the training	• Access to client and field • Time • Expertise for instrument development

Reprinted with permission from Performance Advantage Group, 2004.

Action Plans

Of course, many courses provide action plans for the participants to complete. These can be used as a thread throughout the program, a kind of progressive action plan, or at the end of the course. The intent is for the participant to identify an area, develop strategies and tactics to implement the concept, identify resources needed, and determine a timeframe for completion (figure 6-4). In this case, you are also asked to identify the knowledge and skills required to complete the action plan, which should align with the course objectives.

Figure 6-5 is a template for a team action plan. Here, you are asked to list the team members, the actions with team member accountability, and target dates. You are also asked to identify success criteria, which provide feedback regarding the completion of this action plan.

Figure 6-6 is a representation of Lewin's (1975) force-field analysis approach to action planning. You will most likely model this in your training and then have the participant select an issue, identify the driving and restraining forces, and develop strategies and tactics to strengthen the drivers and minimize or eliminate the restraining forces.

Figure 6-4. A template for an action plan.

| The Action Plan |

The action plan consists of the tactics to accomplish your stated objectives along with the required knowledge and skills.

Objective for which you will develop your tactics:

Tactics to accomplish the objective:	Resources	Date
•		
•		
•		

Knowledge/skills required:

Figure 6-5. Template for a team action plan.

> **Team Action Plan**

Use this form to document your team's action plan and individual commitments.

Objective for which you will develop your actions:

Team Members

1. _____   4. _____
2. _____   5. _____
3. _____   6. _____

Actions (What)	**Person** (Who)	**Target Dates** (When)
1. _____	_____	_____
2. _____	_____	_____
3. _____	_____	_____
4. _____	_____	_____
5. _____	_____	_____
6. _____	_____	_____

Success Criteria _____

_____

Figure 6-6. Template for force-field action planning.

> **Force-Field Action Plan**

Use force-field analysis to shift from the current situation to a future condition.

Subject for change: _____

Driving Forces ◄————————► **Restraining Forces**

——————————————►   ◄——————————————
——————————————►   ◄——————————————
——————————————►   ◄——————————————
——————————————►   ◄——————————————

Strategies

•

•

•

Adapted from Lewin, 1974.

111

These various forms of action plans can be monitored after training. You can request that participants submit their completed actions plans, or you can make this part of your interview process or questions on a survey. In this case, you want to determine the extent to which the participants have implemented their action plans.

Letter to My Manager

Something as simple as a "letter to my manager" can support transfer (figure 6-7). With this document, participants can frame some actions to implement the training content. In the letter, participants identify their actions and request a meeting with their manager to discuss the actions and required resources. Although the participants can complete this during the training and take it to their managers, it would be more powerful if the facilitator would collect these letters and mail them to each participant's manager.

Learning Contract

A learning contract (figure 6-8) supports the development of behavioral competencies. It is often a part of a leadership development initiative. The behaviors to be developed are identified through a 360-degree assessment. The planning for developing a specific competency is done in Part A of the learning contract. A specific competency within a particular context is identified. You also indicate the current assessment level (as determined by the 360-degree assessment) and the desired level of behavior. The gap is the difference between the desired level of behavior and the 360-degree assessment results.

For example, if the 360-degree assessment by peers rated the individual a 2.4 (current) and the position requires a 3.7 (required), the gap is 1.3. The gap is addressed through the development plan. The competency behaviors are the specific behaviors related to the competency needing development. A given competency may encompass from four to six behaviors. Complete the planning section by indicating the required resources, timeframe, and sources of information (sources to monitor progress) to implement the development initiative. The developmental activities can be anything from coaching, to job assignments, to reading, to courses, and so forth.

In Part B, the individual, in collaboration with his or her manager, identifies the things that either or both of them should start, stop, or continue doing to support the developmental effort. This is an important aspect of the development process. Both the manager and the individual are responsible for creating an environment for competency development.

Figure 6-7. Example of a "letter to my manager."

Date: _____

Dear _____:

I have just completed a workshop on evaluation of training programs. The program focused on the transfer of learning from the classroom to the job and determining the impact and ROI of training. During the program, I made some notes on how I can apply the course content to my job. Specifically, I am committing to do the following:

1.

2.

3.

4.

When I return, I would like to meet with you to discuss my commitment and get your reactions and input. Then, upon our agreement on the course of action to take, I will need your support in the following ways:

1.

2.

3.

4.

Signature: _____

Part C is completed at the end of the timeframe, usually at least a year. Another 360-degree assessment is performed and the results compared to the baseline. This feedback indicates the amount of change that has occurred and the new existing gap. There is also space for the individual and the manager to discuss and document the specific behaviors and related situations where the individual demonstrated, or failed to demonstrate, the desired behaviors. After this discussion, Parts A and B are revisited and revised as needed.

Following the program and the completion of the learning contract, you can contact the participant and see how much change has taken place.

Figure 6-8. Learning contract.

Learning Contract

Name _____   Date _____

Part A: Planning (Describe the Improvement Plan)

Goal Statement: "To consistently demonstrate _____ competency

_____ by _____ ."
situations   date

_____ in _____

Assessment level
Current _____
Required _____
Gap _____

Competency Behaviors:	Learning Activity (courses, readings, assignments, and so forth):	Resources:	Timeframe:	Sources of Information

Part B: Professional and Manager Roles (Discuss development roles [for example, seek feedback, refocus efforts/remove obstacles, be accessible] and document manager and professional contributions)

Professional   "To help in achieving the planned development (Page 1, Part A), I will . . ."

Start/Do More Often/Do Better	Continue To	Stop/Do Less Of

Manager   "To help in achieving the planned development (Page 1, Part A), I will . . ."

Start/Do More Often/Do Better	Continue To	Stop/Do Less Of

(continued on page 116)

Figure 6-8. Learning contract (continued).

Part C: Review (Describe observable, documented outcomes from developmental efforts)

Behaviors:

Situations:

Target Level

New Assessment level

Baseline: _____

New Gap _____

Employee _____
signature

_____
date

Manager _____
signature

_____
date

Questionnaires and Surveys

For level 3, you can use a questionnaire or survey to collect data about transfer. One format is a scaled instrument. Because you are asking questions or making statements regarding the perceived use of the knowledge, skills, and abilities on the job and the job environment, consider using such dimensions as degree of agreement ("strongly disagree" to "strongly agree") or the extent to which transfer took place ("not at all" to "a very great extent"). You could list the course objectives that relate to application on the job and inquire about the extent to which each objective has been fulfilled. You could also provide a yes/no checklist indicating whether the participant is using the new knowledge, skills, and abilities on the job.

This approach does not provide you with much information about the extent of the use or the quality or correctness of use; neither does it indicate how much of the training is being used on the job. You could use open-ended questions to allow the participant to complete a question, but these responses are hard to quantify and take some time and skill to analyze.

Interviews

You can conduct interviews with the participants or with their managers, peers, and relevant others. The interview format could be structured and supported with a protocol to allow you to get answers to the same questions when conducting multiple interviews. This format may also allow for asking follow-up questions or probing for clarification. Be sure that you have trained interviewers and that the participants know the purpose and format of the interview and the use of the information.

Focus Groups

A focus group comprising a few people (four to six) can follow a format similar to that as the interview. The advantage here is that others can expand upon ideas expressed by someone else. The focus group may include participants, their managers, or their peers. Be aware that heterogeneous groups that include participants and their managers may inhibit complete expression of ideas on performance. Again, a protocol, the listing of questions, would be a good idea.

Observation

You could also conduct some observation: the less intrusive, the better. As you can imagine, someone sitting next to a former participant can bias the performance of the person being observed. The observation would need to be supported by a checklist or scaled instrument to ensure consistent evaluation. Observation is not always a person sitting observing a performer. Observation can also be done via video cameras or audio recordings as is often the case for telemarketers and customer service reps. Computer monitoring is often used in call centers.

A special type of observation is the use of a mystery shopper. In this type of observation, the evaluator poses as a customer and engages the participant doing his or her job. The trained evaluator has a performance instrument based on the standards for the job and training content. The evaluator then rates the performance of the participant.

Make Transfer Part of Your Organization's Processes

Ideally, your application-to-the-job strategy will become embedded into the organization's processes. For example, an account management program was developed for a major telecommunications company. As part of the training, the participants developed account plans based on customer case studies. This account plan format became the standard for the company. Following the program, any sales professional submitting an account plan had to use the format taught in the program. As an assessor, you could have easily found out how many of the sales professionals were using the format. With the help of the sales manager, you could also evaluate the quality and completeness of the account plans.

This example demonstrates the opportunity to link the training to the company's processes. In this case, the account management format became part of the account planning process. The sales professionals receiving the training are taught the format. They practice using the format in developing account plans using the case study method (based on actual customers). During the training, their case

Noted

If your needs assessment included an analysis of performance records/reviews, have identified weaknesses been addressed? This information is best obtained from the participant's manager. Be careful not to collect confidential information that is not related to the use of training on the job. You only want to know if the weaknesses targeted for improvement through your training program are no longer weaknesses. If there is still a performance problem based on knowledge, skills, and abilities, did the identified weaknesses diminish at least?

responses are evaluated for completeness and quality. This same instrument can now be used for level 3 assessment.

The Effect of Environment

As part of level 3 evaluation, you must also explore the environment. You can use the same instruments and methods discussed earlier, but just ask questions around the work environment. You can develop yes/no or Likert-scale instruments using degree of agreement/disagreement, extent to which the requirement was met, or completion format. You can ask such questions as these:

▶ To what extent were adequate resources provided to support the use of the new knowledge, skills, and abilities on your job or to fulfill your performance contract or action plan?

▶ Did you have time to practice and use your new knowledge, skills, and abilities on your job?

▶ Did you have the consistent opportunity to use the new knowledge, skills, and abilities on your job?

▶ To what extent did you receive coaching and feedback?

▶ How was the use of the new knowledge, skills, and abilities on the job recognized and rewarded?

▶ Did your training receive adequate reinforcement?

▶ Did you have the tools and equipment to use the new knowledge, skills, and abilities on your job?

Think About This

If the participant audience is large, you could take a random sample from the participants, managers, or peers to reduce the amount of analysis required while still maintaining the integrity of the findings.

When selecting an instrument or method, you should weigh such factors as the time available, budget constraints, degree of management and client support, type of data to be collected, how intrusive it is to go into the workplace, and the culture of the organization.

Getting It Done

Transfer to the job is critical to helping your participants and clients meet their objectives. As discussed in this chapter, there are several ways you can increase the probability that transfer will take place. To make this happen, it takes the HRD staff, the manager, peers, and the participant. Transfer then supports level 4 evaluation (impact and ROI).

First, complete the evaluation plan through level 3 for one of your courses using the matrix provided in exercise 6-1.

Next, take some time to evaluate one of your own training courses in terms of how well it is designed to ensure transfer. You may use the instrument provided in figure 6-1. If you don't wish to write in this book, feel free to make a photocopy for your own use.

Now that you have an understanding of level 1 (reaction), level 2 (evaluation for knowledge and application of skills and behaviors within the training setting), and level 3 (use on the job and the environment), you are ready to embark on level 4 to evaluate both the impact and ROI of a training course.

Exercise 6-1. Level 1, 2, and 3 evaluation plan.

Evaluation Plan: Level 1 (Reaction), Level 2 (Learning and Application), and Level 3 (Transfer and Environment)

Business Metric(s): _____

	What	Why	How	Sources	When	Where	Who
Level 1 Reaction							
Level 2 Learning							
Level 2 Application							

(continued on page 122)

Exercise 6-1. Level 1, 2, and 3 evaluation plan (continued).

	What	Why	How	Sources	When	Where	Who
Level 3 Transfer							
Level 3 Environment							

Reprinted with permission from Performance Advantage Group, 2004.

7

Level 4:
Impact and ROI

What's Inside This Chapter

In this chapter, you'll learn:

▶ A working definition of level 4 evaluation
▶ Benefits of conducting level 4 evaluation
▶ Questions clients ask
▶ Organizational drivers for ROI
▶ Guidelines for level 4 evaluation
▶ Eight steps for conducting an impact and ROI analysis
▶ How to develop a communication plan.

A Working Definition of Level 4 Evaluation

Level 4 evaluation is the process of determining the final business results that occurred as a result of the training. It is the process of determining how much the training contributed to the shift in the business metric identified in the initial business analysis and recorded on the evaluation plan. The impact is the actual shift in the business metric. For example, if the training is designed to increase unit sales, the impact is the change in unit sales attributable to the training program. It is important to remember that it's not likely that all the sales increase is due to the training program. Other factors within and outside the organization may have contributed to increase in sales. Impact is *only* the increase in sales due to the participants' involvement in the training program and the transfer of their knowledge, skills, and abilities to the job.

Basic Rule 18
An important part of level 4 evaluation is isolating the effect of the training from other factors that may have affected the business metric.

ROI is the return on the investment in the training. In other words, it is a gauge of how much additional net dollar benefit accrued to the organization for each dollar spent on the training. ROI is usually calculated on an annual basis. If the training program's ROI is 100 percent, it means that for every dollar invested in the training program, one dollar is returned to the organization in net benefits. This means that the program paid for itself but did not add any additional benefits to the organization. If the ROI is above 100 percent, the training made a profit; an ROI under 100 percent means a loss.

The calculation of a ROI is based on two assumptions:

1. *That the business metric can be converted to monetary value:* For example, in the foregoing example, you would need to know the dollar value to the organization for each additional unit sold.
2. *That you can determine the total cost (to be discussed later) of designing, developing, delivering, and evaluating the entire training program:* The entire training program includes any pre-course work or planning sessions, the actual training sessions, and any follow-up sessions or training for reinforcement.

Therefore, the ROI is a matter of comparing the net impact in dollar terms to the total program costs and expressing the ratio as a percentage:

$$ROI = \frac{\text{Program Benefits} - \text{Program Costs}}{\text{Program Costs}} \times 100$$

The ROI calculation is usually done for a single delivery of a single course, but that calculation can then be used to study multiple deliveries.

The Challenges of Level 4

Conducting a level 4 evaluation is not an easy undertaking for several reasons. First, there is a considerable time lag between the training and the evaluation. You must wait a suitable time before measuring transfer and tracking the data. Then, the business metric must be measured. Many times that metric is measured by the organization (not you) and the measure is only taken periodically. Therefore, in many instances, it is six to nine months before a level 4 evaluation is conducted.

Second, it is difficult to separate the many variables that could contribute to the shift in the business metric, that is, to isolate the effects of a single variable such as training. In most cases, training is only one factor among several that may have affected any given business metric. Determining the impact of training alone is difficult.

Third, it takes quite a bit of expertise to plan and implement a level 4 evaluation. Level 4 evaluation also requires more resources (time and money) than levels 1–3.

Benefits of Conducting Level 4 Evaluation

There are several benefits to the training organization and to the client of an impact and ROI analysis. First, level 4 evaluation identifies the contribution training makes to the client and the organization. By effectively providing HRD interventions that positively impact client and organizational needs while providing a positive ROI, training makes a bottom-line contribution. Second, through the ROI analysis, you determine if the cost of the training is justified by the benefits derived from that training. A positive ROI is a good measure for this.

Think About This

The issue is not just getting a positive ROI. The ROI needs to be significant enough to warrant the opportunity costs. For example, if the ROI is 105 percent, the return is marginal. Management could easily make a greater return by investing its dollars in another initiative. Therefore, training ROIs are compared against other investment opportunities that might yield more bang for the buck.

Third, an ROI analysis can help to determine if the training intervention was the most cost-effective solution to the performance problem. Here, the ROI figure

Basic Rule 19

A positive ROI is not enough. You need a significantly positive ROI in the minds of the decision makers.

is important for comparisons, but your total cost figure is also important. Can you get the same or comparative results in a more cost-effective manner? This links to the fourth benefit, the ability to know the total program costs. By knowing these costs, you can manage the project and find ways to be more cost effective.

Next, the ROI can help to prioritize the development (by forecasting ROI) and the continuation of training programs. Generally, programs with the highest forecasted ROI will receive continued funding and support.

Noted

Many programs do not return a positive ROI but are continually offered. In some cases, the decision is made to run a program even at a loss. For example, first aid training would most likely not have a positive ROI (unless a trainee actually saves a life, in which case it would be necessary, from an ROI perspective, to determine the value of that life). There are other programs with the same intent, that is providing skills but with the hope that they will not be needed.

Fifth, level 4 evaluation demonstrates some business savvy on the part of the training organization. This adds credibility with your client and line management.

Questions Clients Ask

You'll likely recall from an earlier chapter that one of the excuses for not doing extensive evaluations was that nobody was asking for them. The assumption is that if nobody verbalizes the request or asks questions, then no questions exist. This is probably a false assumption. Your clients spend considerable resources supporting the training initiatives of their company. Therefore, your clients are asking (though maybe not verbalizing to the training organization) some of the following questions:

▶ What did I get for my money (investment)?
▶ Did my people learn anything?

▸ What difference is the training making to the achievement of my (the client's) objectives?

▸ Are my people using their new knowledge and skills?

▸ What is the training costing the organization?

▸ What is the ROI?

▸ Did the training meet its stated objectives?

▸ How much of the training is actually being used on the job?

▸ What tangible benefits did the organization derive from the training?

▸ Was the training delivered in the most cost-effective way?

▸ How long is the training? Why does it need to be that long?

▸ Is the training customized to our organization or is it off-the-shelf?

▸ Who owns the training material?

Your client is probably asking all of these questions—and more. The response to these questions can come from the evaluation of your courses. Realize that most of the these questions are directed at level 4 evaluation in that they have impact, ROI, and cost implications.

Organizational Drivers for ROI

Why is it important that you be able to conduct a level 4 evaluation? What are the organizational drivers that make this important to the training organization? There are several.

As budgets shrink, it becomes more important that the training organization be able to demonstrate its value to its clients and the organization. Helping your client achieve his or her objectives is a good way to demonstrate value. Providing a realistic ROI is another way to demonstrate value. By demonstrating value, you reduce the chance of losing precious resources. As budgets grow, there is more internal competition for those dollars. Again, by demonstrating value, you are in a better position to get some of those budget dollars.

Whether voiced or not, management is requesting the results of training. You must respond to these requests.

Also, as the training organization becomes more linked to the business strategies of their clients, it comes under increasing pressure for accountability for results. The continued trend toward outsourcing also increases pressure for accountability. As companies focus on their core competencies, their support organizations must also be accountable for cost-effective delivery of services that support those core competencies.

There is now a greater recognition that the only sustainable competitive advantage is an organization's human capital. The development and management of human capital is critical for long-term success. This is squarely in the arena of HRD. The training organization must not only help the organization build its bench strength, but also must help build and manage corporate human competence. So, the pressure is on to demonstrate value and be held accountable for the use of resources.

Guidelines for Level 4 Evaluation

There are a few guidelines to follow in conducting a level 4 evaluation. Some of these are:

- ▶ Conduct all previous levels of evaluation (levels 1–3).
- ▶ Allow enough time for the environment to take effect and for the achievement of business results.
- ▶ Demonstrate the causal link between the business metric from the business analysis or needs assessment and the training.
- ▶ If you can, measure both before and after the training. The before measurement gives you the baseline performance data, and the after measurement provides the change in the business metric.
- ▶ Continue to track the movement of the business metric.
- ▶ Conduct no more analysis than is needed to make your decisions.
- ▶ Isolate the variables; that is, determine the effects of training vis-à-vis other factors on the change in the business metric.
- ▶ If possible, use control groups to help isolate the variables.
- ▶ Determine the monetary value of the change in the business metric.
- ▶ Determine total program costs.
- ▶ You must be able to put the business metric (the benefit) in monetary terms.
- ▶ Use appropriate statistical analysis.
- ▶ Select appropriate programs for level 4 evaluation (table 7-1).

Think About This

Not all training programs need to be evaluated at level 4. In reality, only a small percentage of your courses would fit the criteria for level 4 evaluation. Given the time and cost involved, it is important to select the right training programs for this intense evaluation.

Table 7-1. Training program criteria for level 4 evaluation.

Criterion	What You Need to Consider
Long Life	How long will this training course be offered? The longer the time, the stronger the case for level 4 evaluation.
Very Important	How important is this program in meeting the organization's goals? Is the course part of a strategic initiative? If so, you may want to consider level 4 evaluation.
Link to Program Objectives	Do the program's learning objectives state what is to be implemented and the change in the business metric? You want alignment among business metrics, statement of objectives, and the measurement.
High Cost	The higher the cost of program design, development, and implementation, the greater the need for level 4 evaluation.
Highly Visible	How visible is the program to senior management? The greater the visibility, the greater the likelihood that it is a good candidate for level 4 evaluation.
Large Target Audience	The larger the size of the target audience, the stronger the case for level 4 evaluation.
Data Readily Available	Is the business metric currently being tracked? Would it be a simple matter to collect the data for level 4 evaluation? If the data is not readily available or very difficult or expensive to obtain, you may not want to conduct a level 4 evaluation.
Mandatory Participation	Everyone in the organization being required to attend supports the need for level 4 evaluation.
Executive Request	If an executive is requesting the information, you will need to respond.
Levels 1–3 Evaluation Already Conducted	Have previous levels (1–3) of evaluation been carried out? If not, you will need to conduct a comprehensive evaluation of the training course.
Direct Cause and Effect	How direct is the connection or link between the training program and the business metric? The more the direct linkage, the stronger the case for level 4 evaluation.
Easy Conversion to Monetary Value	If it would be straightforward to convert the business metric to a monetary value, this fact builds a case for level 4 evaluation.

Steps in Conducting an Impact and ROI Analysis

There are eight steps to completing an impact and ROI analysis (figure 7-1). Some of these steps were mentioned previously, but they will be discussed here in somewhat greater detail and in the overarching context of level 4 evaluation.

Step 1: Conduct Business/Needs Analysis

The actual impact and ROI analysis process begins with the business/needs analysis, the identification of the business metric, determining the value of that metric, and the setting of learning objectives. Barksdale and Lund (2001) provide several examples of business metrics, some of which are listed in table 7-2.

Step 2: Develop an Evaluation Strategy and Plan

For level 4 evaluation, you need to complete the evaluation plan for all four levels. Be as complete as possible. Refer to the section in chapter 3 on "Developing the Evaluation Plan" for details.

Figure 7-1. Steps in conducting an impact and ROI analysis.

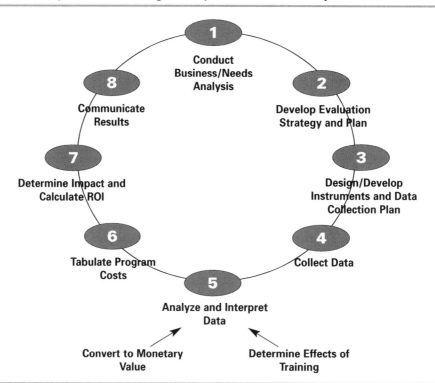

Table 7-2. Common measures to determine effectiveness.

Type of Measure	Potential Measure	Type of Measure	Potential Measure
Operations	• Revenue per employee • Time to delivery • Warranty claims • Cycle time • Returns • Unit costs • Scrap • Rejects • Number of accidents • Errors • Error rates • Defect-free products or parts	Customer	• Customer acquisition • Customer profitability • Customer retention • Customer satisfaction
Productivity	• Number of calls answered • Response time to inquiry • Throughput time	Employees	• Problem resolution • Safety incident rate • Delivery time • Employee satisfaction • Yield per employee • Overtime • Efficiency • Productivity
Management	• Employee retention • Employee satisfaction • Budget goals met • Safety goals met • Employee profitability • Employee lawsuits • Absenteeism • Tardiness • Turnover	Innovation and Creativity	• Product launch success • Product development • Suggestions for improvement
Financial	• Operating income growth • Sales per employee • Revenue generated • Expenses as percentage of sales • Expense ratio • Budget variance • Financial penalties • Inventory turnover	Marketing and Sales	• Revenue per employee • Market share • Improved delivery • Cross-sell ratio • Percentage revenue from new product

Step 3: Design and Develop Instruments and Data Collection Plan

In this step, you actually design and develop the instruments and methods for data collection. In some cases, the instruments—action plans, performance contracts, and so forth—are already a part of the program design.

In other cases, you must develop the instruments (surveys, questionnaires, interview and focus group protocols, for example). These methods were presented in earlier chapters; there may be some nuances related to level 4 evaluation in order to collect information about costs, perceived value of the training, and so forth. For example, let's say that you elect to develop a survey or a questionnaire. At level 4, you may want to include a reliability or confidence level. The reliability or confidence level represents the degree of confidence that the responders' estimates provided for the organizational impact are accurate. (This is discussed in more detail in step 5.) The respondents indicate their degree of confidence by assigning a percentage to their confidence in their estimate. A 100 percent confidence level indicates that they are completely confident that their estimate is accurate.

Noted

Jack Phillips popularized the concept of collecting data on confidence levels for the purposes of level 4 evaluation. The Additional Resources section of this book lists some of his publications on this topic.

Basic Rule 20

Although you want to get information from multiple sources (participant, supervisor, manager), be sure to get the information from those closest to the data sought.

Another option is collecting data through interviews and focus groups. Again, you may want to include a discussion of other factors that might affect the results and use the estimate and confidence methods previously mentioned. Other methods include the follow-up on action plans, performance contracts, observation, and performance tracking.

Performance tracking allows you to determine a baseline of performance prior to training. The performance is continually tracked until you conduct your level 4 evaluation. At that time, the difference between the pretraining baseline and the current performance is the effect of training. This is simply a pre/post measurement. Again, you must take into consideration other factors that could have impacted the performance (isolation of variables).

A variation of performance tracking is the trend-line approach. Using previous information (collected at least six months prior to the training intervention if possible), you draw (plot) a baseline of the data and extend it into the future (beyond the point of the training intervention). Following the training, the actual performance data is plotted and compared to the original extended line. The difference between the two lines is the change in performance, some or all of which is likely attributable to training. Again, you need to isolate the variables to determine exactly how much of the performance change is due to training. See step 5 for more detail on isolation of variables.

Think About This

For the initial trend-line, you plot the data and then statistically determine the line of best fit. This line is then extended into the future. The trend-line method assumes that the forces driving the initial trend-line will stay in place and have the same intensity of impact on performance. In essence, the future (extended trend-line) is subject to the same forces as the initial baseline. This is a huge assumption; that's why it is important to collect information about confidence levels and to always use the most conservative numbers. Being upfront about your assumptions and confidence levels is the way to build your credibility in the organization.

You may elect to use a control group to conduct your level 4 evaluation. Again, this decision was made when you developed the evaluation plan. In the control group design, one group receives the training (experimental) and the other group (control) does not. You then compare the groups' performance following training. Ideally, the groups need to

- be demographically similar
- have similar environmental influences or working conditions
- be isolated from each other (no communication)
- have participants of the groups randomly selected.

Step 4: Collect Data

You've made your data collection decisions regarding instruments and methods, identified and developed the instruments, identified the sources of information and the timing and the people who are responsible. Now is the time to implement your data collection plan.

Step 5: Analyze and Interpret Data

Step 5 has two parts. The first part is to determine the effects of training. To do this, you must isolate the variables, that is, identify other non-training factors impacting the change in the business metric. The second part of step 5 involves converting the training benefits to monetary value, that is, determining the dollar value of the benefit.

Isolation of variables is one of the most difficult tasks of evaluation. Some methods include the use of control groups, estimation, and trend-line analysis. Phillips (1997) goes into some detail about how to determine confidence levels and isolate variables.

Control Groups. Using the control group design, one group receives the training (experimental) and the other group (control) does not. Compare the groups' performance following the training, and the benefit is the difference in performance between those receiving the training (experimental) and those not receiving the training (control):

Net Benefit = (Average Trained Performance − Average Untrained [Control] Performance)

The result is then standardized in terms of percentage of job performance improvement. Calculate this by dividing the net benefit by the average untrained group's performance:

Standard Training Impact = Net Benefit ÷ Average Untrained [Control] Performance × 100

An example may help clarify the use of control groups. Suppose there are two groups, Group A and Group B. Group A is the control, and Group B received the training. The comparison of the two groups' performance before and after the training intervention is shown in table 7-3.

With this data, you can now calculate the net benefit of training and the standard training impact:

Table 7-3. Using a control group to measure impact.

Group	Production Pretraining	Intervention	Production Posttraining
Group A	400 units	—	400 units
Group B	400 units	Training	900 units

Net Benefit = Group B Posttraining Performance − Group A [Control] Performance =
900 − 400 = 500

Standard Training Impact = 500 [Net Benefit] ÷ 400 [Group A Posttraining] = 1.25 × 100 =
125% Increase in Production Due to Training

Because the production of Group A remained the same, you can assume that no factors other than training influenced the results.

Think About This

If you just compared Group B before and after the training, this would be a simple pre/post measure. In this case, the results would be the same only because both units began with the same production.

In some instances, production may go up in both groups during the training. This is because something influenced the groups other than training. Table 7-4 provides an example.

Table 7-4. Using a control group: isolation of variables.

Group	Production Pretraining	Intervention	Production Posttraining
Group A	400 units	—	600 units
Group B	400 units	Training	900 units

Net Benefit = 900 − 600 = 300

Standard Training Impact = 300 ÷ 600 = 0.5 × 100 =
50% Increase in Production Due to Training

In this case, something influenced the control group (Group A) and caused the production to increase by 200 units. That "something" cannot be the training intervention because Group A did not receive the intervention. Because of the nature of control groups, you must assume that what ever affected Group A also affected Group B. This influence reduces the impact of training because something other than training influenced production. At this time, you do not know what it is. By discovering the other causal factors(s), you can identify non-training influences on production. This would then allow you to reinforce these other factors, providing even greater increases in production. It is also possible that these other influences may be more cost effective than training.

Use of Estimates. For some reason, many HRD professionals don't put much faith in people's estimates. Yet, it is a fairly common practice. Estimates are based on individuals' experience and expertise and, therefore, are informed estimates. For example, organizations make sales estimates (forecasts), estimates of inventory, even retirement planning every day. The key is to have the people closest to the data and who have the greatest relevant perspective to make the estimates. These individuals are usually the participants, their managers, internal experts, and others.

This method can be used in conjunction with surveys, interviews, or focus groups. When asking people to make estimates, you should ask the following questions:

▶ What percentage of the improvement is due to the training?
▶ How reliable (confident are you) is this figure? What degree of confidence do you have in your estimate? The respondents are to provide a percentage figure, keeping in mind that 100 percent means being fully confident. You can improve the reliability for this method by adding this factor to your research.
▶ What is the basis for your estimate?
▶ What other factors might have contributed to the improvement? This information can help you isolate the variables.

For example, in a focus group you may state that based on the data, turnover in your call center dropped from nine people per quarter to five people per quarter—a decrease of four people per quarter, or 16 people per year. Be sure to annualize the data because ROI is calculated on an annual basis. You would then:

1. Ask the respondents about other major factors (other than training) that might have influenced the decrease in turnover. The process is isolation of variables. Include an "other" category for minor factors affecting the results.

2. Then, ask them to indicate what percentage of the increase was related to each major factor. These percentages should add up to 100 percent.
3. Last, have them indicate how sure (confident) they are about their estimates. Again, these figures are reported as percentages. Because each factor is rated independently, the confidence levels do not have to add up to 100 percent.

You could provide a table for them to complete (table 7-5).

Table 7-5. Confidence levels for decrease in turnover.

Factors	Estimated Contribution of Factor to the Decrease in Turnover	Confidence in Estimate
Training	40%	85%
Career Path and Coaching	58%	90%
Other	2%	98%
Total	100%	—

In this case, the respondent thinks that training was 40 percent responsible for the decrease in turnover. In addition, the respondent has a quite a bit of confidence in that estimate (85 percent). The new benefit is then:

$$\text{Benefit} \times \% \text{ Estimate of Contribution} \times \% \text{ Confidence} = \text{New Benefit}$$

or, in this case:

$$\text{Benefit} \times 40\% \times 85\% = \text{New Benefit}$$

This table also tells you that there was another factor that had a significant impact on the decrease in turnover. In this case, there was an initiative that resulted in developing career paths with coaching to help representatives identify future positions and prepare for a promotion. According to the respondent, the career path and coaching had a greater effect on the decrease in turnover.

Trend-Line Analysis. To track performance, you may use a trend-line approach by which you plot the data over time (time series). You plot the performance data on the X-axis and the timeline on the Y-axis (figure 7-2). The first line to plot is the business

Noted

You can use also this method of estimating confidence levels for multiple respondents. To use it in a focus group, you can have individuals provide their estimates and then you average their input. You could also have them voice their estimate and lead a discussion to gain consensus on the other factors that affect the results, estimates, and reliability/confidence. The voicing of other factors and of estimates and getting consensus results in greater ownership and credibility of the data.

metric using extant data, reflecting the movement of the business metric up to the point of the training (line A to A1). It is good to have at least six months of prior data on which to base your trend-line. You may need to use historical data for this. Then, statistically determine the line of best fit and extend that line into the future to the point when you conduct your level 4 evaluation (line A1 to A2). This line represents the continuation of the business metric if there had been no training intervention. Line A1 to A2 is simply the extension of line A to A1.

Following the training intervention, continue to track and plot the business metric. At the time of the level 4 evaluation, you statistically determine the line of best fit for the data points from the time of the training intervention to the time of the evaluation, line A1 to B. The vertical difference between the data points at A2 and B represents the difference due to training—the training impact. Again, you must isolate training's effect from the effect of other variables that could have impacted the business metric. A review of statistical tools and methods is beyond the scope of this book. You can get SPSS software packages that will help with your analysis. Also, see Makridakis's (1989) book, *Forecasting Methods for Management.*

The second part of step 5 is to convert the training benefits to monetary value by determining the dollar value of the benefit. This should be straightforward, based on the business analysis. While working with the client, you determined the business metric *and* the dollar value of that metric. For example, you would have determined the cost of turnover for the call center. You would have an average cost figure related to each person leaving the call center. For example, each representative leaving the call center represents a cost of $22,500. This is the total cost of turnover for one person leaving. If your training intervention is designed to reduce defects, you would establish with the client the cost of each defect.

Figure 7-2. Example of trend-line analysis.

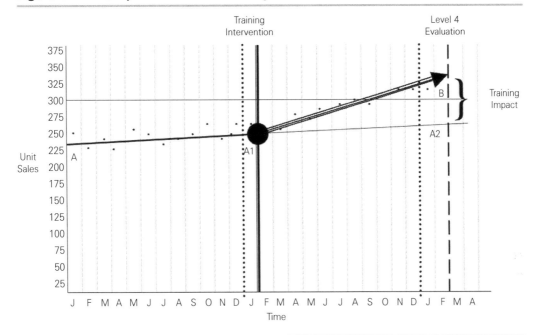

Noted

To isolate the effect of training from the effect of other factors, you combine two methods, including the use of estimates. For example, when completing the trend-line analysis, you have a change in the business metric. You would then use the estimate approach to isolate the effects of the different variables and estimate the contribution of training to the change in the business metric.

Using the previous example, you can now establish the annual savings accruing to the call center by reducing the number of annual turnovers by four (table 7-6). To summarize the situation:

▸ A call center is experiencing turnover of nine people per quarter.
▸ The HRD department conducted a training program to reduce turnover (giving feedback/coaching, setting objectives, resolving complaints/grievances, evaluating performance).

▸ Turnover dropped to five people per quarter, representing a savings of four turnovers per quarter (benefit).

▸ The cost of turnover is $22,500 per person (provided by the client in conjunction with HRD).

▸ The other factor affecting turnover was the implementation of a career path supported by coaching in the call center.

As you can see from table 7-6, the career path and coaching contributed more toward the reduction in turnovers than did the training. Does this mean that the training didn't achieve a positive ROI? Does it mean that the call center should put more resources into career path development and coaching? At this point, you don't know the answer because you don't have the cost information to determine ROI.

Step 6: Tabulate Program Costs

Tabulating program costs involves determining all the costs of the training program and totaling them to get a total cost. But, what constitutes the training program? Does it include pretraining materials? Does it include posttraining follow-up for reinforcement? Does it include job aids? Does it include overhead? Does it include the salaries and benefits of managers for the time spent in the program and any follow-up? The answer to all these questions is yes. Table 7-7 provides a cost worksheet that provides guidance in determining the costs. Be sure to allocate all costs related to the design/development, delivery, and evaluation of the training program. In some cases, your figures may include hourly calculations. You will notice some duplication in items. This allows you to better manage your cost side of training.

Step 7: Determine the Impact and Calculate the ROI

The impact is the shift in the business metric. In the call center example, the impact is the reduction in turnover. ROI goes a step further in that it

▸ determines the associated costs for the training program

▸ isolates the variables to determine the impact training has on the shift in the business metric

▸ determines the dollar value of the benefit

▸ completes the calculation:

$$\text{ROI} = \frac{\text{Program Benefits} - \text{Program Costs} \times 100}{\text{Program Costs}}$$

Table 7-6. Estimated impact of different variables on turnover costs for the call center.

Factor	A. Estimated Contribution of Factor to the Decrease in Turnover	B Confidence in Estimate	C $ Impact (Cost x A x B)	D Impact per Quarter (C x 4 turnovers saved)	E Annualized $ Impact (D x 4 quarters)
Training	40%	85%	$22.5K × 40% × 85% = $7,650/person/qtr	$30,600	$122,400
Career Path and Coaching	58%	90%	$22.5K × 58% × 85% = $11,745/person/qtr	$46,980	$187,920
Other	2%	98%	$22.5K × 2% × 85% = $441/person/qtr	$1,764	$7,056
Totals	100%	—	—	—	—

Table 7-7. Program cost worksheet.

NEEDS ASSESSMENT COSTS	Cost
• Salaries plus benefits of HRD staff	$
• Salaries plus benefits of participants involved in needs assessment	
• Contractor's fees plus expenses	
— Travel and living	
— Office supplies	
— Printing expenses	
— Shipping	
— Equipment expense	
— Overhead allocation	
— Miscellaneous expenses	
Subtotal	$
DESIGN AND DEVELOPMENT COSTS	
• Salaries plus benefits of HRD staff	$
• Salaries plus benefits of participants, peers, and managers involved in design/development	
• Travel and living of peers and managers involved	
• Contractor's fees plus expenses	
• Office supplies	
• Participants' materials	
— Manual	
— Tests and instruments	
— Pre-read materials	
— Job aids	
— Post-program materials and readings	
— Facilitator guide	
• Media	
— Videos	
— Overheads or transparencies	
— 35 mm slides	
— Films	
— Audiotapes	
— CDs	

DESIGN AND DEVELOPMENT COSTS (continued)	
— Wallboards	
— Flipcharts	
— Artwork	
— Copyrights	
— Royalties	
— Shipping	
• Equipment expenses	
• Other services	
• Overhead allocation	
• Miscellaneous expenses	
Subtotal	$
DELIVERY COSTS	
• Facilitators' salaries plus expenses	$
• Facilitators' travel and living	
• Other presenters' salaries plus expenses	
• Other presenters' travel and living	
• External/vendors' facilitator fees	
— External/vendors' travel and living	
— On-the-job coaches' salary and benefits	
• HRD support staff salary and benefits	
• Participants' travel and living	
• Costs for others taking over participants' work	
• Registration expenses	
• Opportunity cost	
• Meals and breaks	
• Facility expenses	
• Equipment expenses (including software)	
• Shipping	
• Materials and supplies	
• Overhead allocation	
• Miscellaneous expenses	
Subtotal	$

(continued on page 144)

Table 7-7. Program cost worksheet (continued).

EVALUATION COSTS	
• Salary and benefits of HRD staff	$
• Travel and living	
• Salary and benefits of participants	
• Salary and benefits of managers and peers	
• Contractor's fees plus expenses	
• Printing	
• Other services	
• Office supplies and expenses	
• Equipment expenses	
• Overhead allocation	
• Miscellaneous expenses	
Subtotal	$
GRAND TOTAL	**$**

Reprinted with permission from Performance Advantage Group, 2004.

Think About This

You determine the value of the business metric in collaboration with the client. This approach secures the client's buy-in and helps answer any questions later regarding the legitimacy of the benefit data.

ROI, then, is the return on the investment in training. It represents how much additional net dollar benefit accrued to the organization for each dollar spent on the training. Remember that anything over 100 percent adds positive dollar value to the organization. So, a ROI of 112 percent means that for each dollar spent on training, the organization received $12 in return.

Going back to the call center example, you already know that the annual dollar value of the benefit from a reduction of four turnovers per quarter is $122,400. Assume that the course was a two-day initiative and that the total cost was $45,250. The ROI is:

$$\frac{\text{Program Benefits} - \text{Program Costs}}{\text{Total Course Costs}} \times 100 = \frac{\$122,400 - \$45,250}{\$45,250} \times 100 = 170.45\%$$

That is, for each dollar spent on this training, the organization gets a return of $70.45.

Step 8: Communicate the Results

Who is interested in what information? Not all information is of equal value to all audiences. Generally, the HRD staff is most interested in level 1 data. This is information available immediately following the training intervention. At this time, the HRD staff is getting ready for the next delivery so this information is very timely. The HRD staff can look at the information and make some decisions before the next delivery regarding delivery strategies, learning activities, modifying or emphasizing content. In other cases, the information focuses on where the HRD staff may need to gather additional information.

Level 2 information is primarily for the HRD staff and managers of the participants. The immediate results on tests and assessments are provided to participants as feedback on their learning and practice. The HRD staff uses this information for program revision (content and instructional strategies) and decisions around the quality of facilitation. Also, the managers of the participants really want to know if their employees learned anything as a result of their investment: Did learning take place? Were the participants able to demonstrate the skills? Have participants' abilities improved?

Noted

The information from level 2 evaluation can be shared with the managers of the participants on an aggregate basis. This provides them with information related to learning and demonstration of knowledge, skills, and abilities in the training course. At the same time, it allows for anonymity for the participants. It is up to the participant to share any specific assessment information with his or her manager.

The primary audience for level 3 is the participants' managers. Because they are sending their people to the training, they want to know if it transfers to the job. What is the utility of the training? Is the training being used on the job? If so, how much of the training is being transferred? They also want to know of any barriers to transfer so they can take action to minimize or remove these barriers. Likewise, they want to know what enablers to reinforce to enhance transfer.

This does not mean that the HRD staff isn't interested in level 3 evaluation. There is rich information regarding how to improve transfer through better design, involvement of the field in the design/development process, and facilitation of the training. Although environmental issues have some HRD implications, there are also non-training issues that affect transfer. Identifying these issues and sharing that information with appropriate people (managers and others in HR) can help build a more supportive environment.

The client would be interested in level 3 to get an insight into the potential change that could support his or her objectives. If transfer takes place and the business metric moves in a positive direction, your client receives help and benefits. The client's workforce is improving in those areas—that's good news! Alternatively, if transfer does not take place, the client can help identify and implement training and non-training strategies to make a positive change in the environment.

Level 4 evaluation results are of great interest to your client. The client invested heavily in the training initiative. Even if the training is a corporate-sponsored program, managers still send their employees and help fund it. So, clients want to know what they are getting for their investment (ROI). They want to know the extent to which the business metric moved (impact). They want to know how the training can be provided more cost effectively. This information comes from the training cost analysis. Your client wants to know if the training was cost effective. Level 4 evaluation provides this information.

Your HRD line managers are also interested in level 4 results. They build and sustain relationships with their clients and must seek continued funding for HRD initiatives. Positive and significant impact and ROI help position them to do this. It's clear that different audiences are interested in different information. Therefore, the following guidelines provide assistance:

- ▶ Align the information with the interests and needs of the target audience.
- ▶ Provide the complete information in a concise format.
- ▶ Provide the information in a timely manner so that your client or HRD management can use it to make relevant decisions.
- ▶ Make recommendations based on the research results.

▶ Communicate the information in an objective fashion. This is a research report and should not contain biased opinions or exaggerations.

▶ Provide an executive summary containing the most important information and recommendations.

▶ Present the information in an appropriate format for the audience. This could be a written report, verbal discussion, presentation supported by media, executive format, and so forth.

 Getting It Done

Chapter 7 introduced you to the world of level 4 evaluation—impact and ROI. Level 4 data can show how much the training contributed to the shift in the business metric identified in the initial business analysis and recorded on the evaluation plan. Certainly, carrying out high-level evaluation involves challenges for the HRD department, but the process positions the department as a strategic partner of the client.

Exercise 7-1 can help you think about building upon the evaluation plan for one of your courses to include level 4 evaluation.

Exercise 7-2 presents a case study. See if you can determine the ROI for the meeting management training program. The solution follows the exercise.

Exercise 7-1. Level 1, 2, 3, and 4 evaluation plan.

Evaluation Plan: Level 1 (Reaction), Level 2 (Learning and Application), Level 3 (Transfer and Environment), and Level 4 (Impact and ROI)

Business Metric(s): _____

	What	Why	How	Sources	When	Where	Who
Level 1 Reaction							
Level 2 Learning							
Level 2 Application							

	What	Why	How	Sources	When	Where	Who
Level 3 Transfer							
Level 3 Environment							
Level 4 Impact							
Level 4 ROI							

Exercise 7-2. Calculating ROI: a case study.

Meeting Management

Communications R Us (a fictitious company) is a manufacturing organization producing components for car stereos and CD players. The organization has 4,000 employees, including 35 supervisors. Middle management has noticed that some supervisors appear to be spending an inordinate amount of time in meetings. This situation has adversely affected their time to do some operational aspects of their jobs and focus on their people who need coaching. The middle managers contacted you, the training specialist, to help reduce the amount of time supervisors are spending in meetings.

In response to their request, you developed a time log for supervisors. All 35 supervisors logged their time in meetings for a month. It was determined that there were two distinct groupings. Fifteen managers spent between six and nine hours in formal meetings during a month. The remaining 20 managers averaged 20 hours per month in meetings. When correlating performance against the managers, it was also discovered that the managers spending less time in meetings were also performing better overall.

Based on this data, and with the agreement of the middle managers, you designed and delivered a one-day meeting management course. It was provided to the 35 managers in two identical sessions. The 20 managers with excessive time spent in meetings were in one of the two sessions. The sessions were completed four months ago. You have been asked to calculate the ROI on the session involving the 20 managers.

Through data collection you have determined the following information:

- Prior to the training, the 20 managers spent an average of 20 hours per month in meetings.
- The participants' average annual salary is $74,074.
- The company benefit package is valued at 35 percent of salary.
- Following the training, the 20 managers now average eight hours per month in meetings.

To calculate ROI, you must first determine the program costs. Use these assumptions to complete the table that follows:

- There are 240 workdays in a year.
- There are 1,920 hours in a work year.
- A workday is eight hours.
- Two days of administrative support is required for each offering.

Meeting Management Training Program Costs	Cost per Session
Program design and development was $17,000	
Facilitation (assume no preparation time) (annual fully loaded salary of $65,000)	
Participant time	
Materials ($35/participant)	
Administrative support (annual fully loaded salary of $45,000)	
TOTAL COST	

Based on the information provided and the following equation, what is the ROI for the one session?

$$ROI = \frac{\text{Program Benefits} - \text{Program Costs}}{\text{Total Program Costs}} \times 100 = \underline{\hspace{2cm}} \%$$

Solution to exercise 7-2.

Program Costs

Meeting Management Training Program Costs	Cost per Session
Program design and development was $17,000	$8,500 (prorated)
Facilitation (assume no preparation time) (annual fully loaded salary of $65,000)	$271 $65K/240 days
Participant time	$8,320 ($100K/240 days = $416/day × 20 participants)
Materials ($35/participant)	$700 ($35 × 20 participants)
Administrative support (annual fully loaded salary of $45,000)	$375 ($45K/240 days × 2 days)
TOTAL COST	**$18,166***

*May be some differences due to rounding.

Benefit Analysis

- 20 managers were involved in the training and, therefore, in the analysis.
- Each of the 20 managers was spending 20 hours per month in meetings.
- Salary plus benefits was $100,000 per manager.
- Unit value was $52/hr ($100,000 ÷ 1,920hr/yr).
- Cost of meetings was $1,040 per manager ($52 × 20 hr).
- The annualized cost per manager was $12,480 ($1,040 × 12 mo).
- The total annualized cost for the 20 managers was $249,600 ($12,480 × 20 managers).

The intervention was a one-day meeting management skills workshop, with the following results:

- Each manager is now spending eight hours per month in meetings.
- The new cost of meetings is $416 per month per manager ($52/hr × 8 hr).
- The annualized cost per manager is $4,992 ($416 × 12 mo).
- The total annualized cost for the 20 managers is now $99,840 ($4,992 × 20 managers).
- The benefit savings is $624 per month per manager ($1,040 − $416) or $7,488 per manager per year ($624 × 12 mo).
- The total annualized benefit for the 20 managers is $149,760 ($7,488 × 20 managers).
  or
- Benefit of 12 hr/manager/mo (20 hr − 8 hr).
- Dollar value of the benefit is $149,760 ($52/hr × 12 hr × 12 mo × 20 managers).

$$\text{ROI} = \frac{\text{Program Benefits} - \text{Program Costs}}{\text{Total Program Costs}} \times 100 = \frac{\$149,760 - \$18,166}{\$18,166} \times 100 = \mathbf{724.40\%}$$

This chapter presented a step-by-step process for conducting an impact and ROI analysis. Exercise 7-2 gave you the opportunity to practice determining an ROI. This chapter also presented some guidelines for communicating evaluation results in accordance with audience needs. This information provides a basis for developing a communication plan, a process that is discussed in chapter 8.

8

Evaluation Biases and Communicating the Results

What's Inside This Chapter

In this chapter, you'll learn:

▶ Kinds and implications of bias
▶ The components of an evaluation report
▶ How to develop a communication plan.

Kinds and Implications of Bias

The original development of your research methods and instruments is subject to several types of bias. Sources of bias cut across all four levels of evaluation.

Although it is difficult to address bias, it is not impossible. First, recognize that bias exists and then take action to minimize it. Take steps to discern the types of bias that might be present and acknowledge them in your communications. That way, you can build your credibility by taking an appropriate, conservative approach when you present the results of your evaluation. Biased information or the failure to acknowledge sources of bias can taint your results and calls into question the credibility of the evaluation effort.

Sampling Bias

The first type of bias is sampling bias. It is easy to send surveys or interview certain participants whom you know and like and who are favorably disposed to the program. There is also a tendency to send the information to recent participants who usually are still enthusiastic about the course and about the opportunity to implement their action plans. The realities of the environment have not dampened their spirits.

These practices can result in tainted data by introducing sampling bias. You should always conduct surveys or interviews with participants selected on a random basis.

Insufficient Sample Size

The second bias comes from not having a large enough sample. Sampling generally applies to levels 3 and 4 evaluation. You draw your sample from the entire population, in this case, all the participants taking a course. The population could be all deliveries of a particular course, from which you randomly select particular deliveries to evaluate.

Depending on the audience size of each delivery, you may randomly select participants from each delivery to be evaluated. For example, if you designed and delivered a sales training course that is delivered twice a month with an average class size of 24 participants, you could randomly select two or three deliveries out of the 24 deliveries. From each delivery, you could then randomly select participants to involve in the evaluation study. A sample that is too small is not representative of the entire population or group. Therefore, statistically determine the size of sample required to provide reliable data.

A discussion of sampling is beyond the scope of this book. However, most basic statistics books discuss sampling methods. Other resources on sampling include SPSS software programs and Makridakis's (1989) book, *Forecasting Methods for Management.*

Think About This

For many HRD professionals, statistics is not a strength. One solution is to use a graduate student to conduct your statistical analysis. This approach provides you with data, but you must still know what the data means in order to interpret it.

Observation Bias

The observation technique is not without bias problems also. The more visible the observation process is, the less reliable the data is. Participants perform differently if they know they are being observed. An observer who is not trained or provided with proper instruments adds to the unreliability of the data. Therefore, conduct your observations in the least obtrusive manner possible while still getting the information you need. Provide training for the observers and use some sort of instrument, such as a checklist, to aid in the observation.

Bias in Interviews and Focus Groups

Interviews and focus groups can provide high-quality information. To be most useful and to avoid bias, the interview design must ensure that

- the sample is representative of the population
- the participants understand the questions
- the participants are willing participants (their participation is not mandatory)
- the interviewer is trained in interviewing techniques and knows how to record the information accurately
- there is a protocol for consistency in questioning
- there is a method to objectively evaluate the results of the interview.

Restriction of Range or Range Error

Some respondents to a survey or questionnaire may engage in the error of restriction or range. This occurs when the respondent, or rater, restricts all his or her ratings to a small section of the rating scale. This could be positive (leniency) or negative (severity).

In some cases, this phenomenon is an unconscious bias on the part of the rater. In other cases, the rater may like (or dislike) going to training. If the rater was required to attend the training, that could lead to a restriction of range on the negative side. These issues can be addressed when the instrument is being completed. If the evaluation is taking place with the participants present, you can have a brief discussion about this. Or, you could include a brief discussion about such rater errors in the instruction section of the instrument.

Bias of Central Tendency

Some people hesitate to commit to either end of the scale and just indicate responses near the middle. This is called the bias of central tendency. For example, if you have a rating scale of 1 to 5, some raters tend to use the middle value of 3. You can address this source of bias by developing a scale with no middle value (1–4).

Emotional Bias

This type of bias impacts level 1 evaluation to the greatest extent. This bias occurs when the participants allow their feelings (like or dislike) for the facilitator to bias their ratings. Liking and disliking are emotions that are directed toward an object or person. In this case, the object of the liking or disliking could be the program or the facilitator. If these emotions go unchecked, they can contaminate the ratings.

This type of bias is difficult to address. One thing that a facilitator can do is to provide interim evaluations to allow participants to express themselves. Any overtly biased perspectives (positive or negative) could then be addressed during the training course.

Components of an Evaluation Report

Before you communicate the evaluation results, you need to write the report. A general format for a more comprehensive report includes the following elements:

▷ executive summary
▷ general information
▷ background information on the client and the program
▷ target audiences for the report
▷ expected outcomes
▷ how the results will be used
▷ format of the study
▷ overview of the levels of evaluation
▷ impact and ROI process
▷ linking impact and ROI to design
▷ training course information
▷ course objectives
▷ course duration and content
▷ course target audience
▷ class size and number of offerings
▷ evaluation and impact/ROI
▷ level 1 analysis
▷ level 2 analysis

- level 3 analysis
- level 4 analysis
- course ROI
- observations and recommendations
- attachments
- the design model
- audience analysis
- data collection forms
- details of data analysis (for example, trend-line estimation).

The Communication Plan

Who gets the results? How do you communicate the results to those interested parties? How much information should you communicate? These are all questions related to developing a communication plan. With the report completed, you need to make decisions regarding who gets what information and in what format. Figure 8-1 presents a model of a communication plan.

Let's take a closer look at the components of the communication plan in figure 8-1:

- *Audience:* Identify the individual to receive a communication. The people in your communication audience could include your client, your line management, participants, facilitators, and others.
- *Message:* Determine what content needs to be included for each audience. Your client may just want an executive summary, but your manager may want the entire report. The message should answer the what question on the evaluation plan.
- *Vehicle:* Determine how the message will be communicated. You may provide a written executive summary and presentation to your client. Your manager may want the complete report plus a briefing. Participants may only receive a summary. The information could be presented in person, in a written format as a report or on a CD, or it could be distributed via email. The vehicle needs to match the audience preference.
- *Desired Result:* Do you want a response from the material? What do you want the reader to do as a result of receiving the message? This should address the why question from the evaluation plan.
- *Timing:* The communication timing needs to align with the timing set down in the evaluation plan (the when column). It also needs to align with when

Figure 8-1. The communication plan.

Audience	Message	Vehicle	Desired Result	Timing	Frequency	Person Responsible

Reprinted with permission from Performance Advantage Group, 2004.

your client, program manager, or HRD manager needs to make his or her decisions regarding the training course.

▶ *Frequency:* How often are you going to communicate with the audience? Will you be making a report after each delivery? Will you be making quarterly reports? Clients sometimes want an update with their quarterly planning sessions.

▶ *Person Responsible:* The evaluator is generally responsible for doing the research and analysis and writing the report. His or her manager may be the person who presents the executive summary to the client. Others may be involved in developing media, editing, and so forth to support the communication.

Basic Rule 21
You must align the message, desired results, timing, and frequency with the audience needs.

The communication plan is not the end of the process. Usually the reader has questions that must be answered. This allows you the opportunity to further develop those relationships and demonstrate how the training initiative can add value to the client.

Getting It Done
This chapter was about communication. You first looked at sources of bias that could affect the credibility of your results. Then, the components of an evaluation report were presented, followed by the development of a communication plan.

You now have the opportunity to identify any biases that may be present in your data collection (exercise 8-1). You can also practice developing a communication plan for one of your evaluation projects. Remember, the communication plan needs to address each audience you want to communicate with.

Exercise 8-1. Identify sources of bias in your evaluation data.

Check off any sources of bias that may be present in your data collection methodology. Then, develop actions to address the bias.

✔	Bias	Actions
	Sampling Bias (Preferred Participants)	
	Sampling Bias (Size)	
	Observation Bias	
	Bias in Interviews and Focus Groups	
	Restriction of Range	
	Central Tendency Bias	
	Emotional Bias (Like or Dislike of Facilitator)	

Using the model in figure 8-1, which is reproduced in exercise 8-2, complete a communication plan for one of your completed evaluation projects.

Exercise 8-2. Complete a communication plan for evaluating one of your courses.

Audience	Message	Vehicle	Desired Result	Timing	Frequency	Person Responsible

Reprinted with permission from Performance Advantage Group, 2004.

This book has discussed many aspects of evaluation including some foundational concepts, evaluation's interrelationship with course design, development of an evaluation plan, and then some detail on all four levels of evaluation, with subparts. To successfully implement these ideas, you must have a relationship with your client, and there must be readiness within your organization. These aspects are addressed in the final chapter.

A Final Thought

What's Inside This Chapter

In this chapter, you'll:

▶ Revisit the link between design and evaluation
▶ Learn ways to demonstrate value to your client
▶ Explore the readiness of your organization for conducting more extensive evaluations.

Design and Evaluation

Evaluation is not an activity to be developed at the conclusion of the design/development process, nor is it something that is completed at the end of a course delivery. Evaluation is part of the training program; instructional design is incomplete without evaluation. Evaluation should be planned before the program activities are designed.

When you have your initial conversations with your client regarding a training initiative, you should be discussing a critical aspect of evaluation—the business metric. The purpose of the training is to close the identified gap in the business metric: the difference between where the client is and where he or she wants to be. Without a business metric, there is no data to track to measure the performance change.

During this business analysis phase of design, you will also want to

- determine the value of the business metric
- determine how to track the business metric
- explore ways to gather input from the field
- emphasize the critical nature of field support
- discuss the extent of the evaluation effort (to what level of evaluation)
- discuss the what and why aspects of the evaluation plan.

The evaluation plan sets forth the details of how you will conduct your course evaluation. Complete the evaluation plan to the level the client (or your manager) wants that course evaluated. Discuss the completed evaluation plan with your client and your manager, if appropriate. Again, field input and support are critical to gather information for transfer and assessment of the environment. Be sure to get access to the field. Also, be sure there is a data tracking mechanism in place to monitor the shift in the business metric if you are conducting a level 4 evaluation.

Another strong link between design and evaluation is the learning objectives. These must be stated in measurable terms and to the level to which the training course will be evaluated. For level 2, objectives need to reflect knowledge and application (within the training program), such as "list" or "recognize" or "demonstrate" or "identify." For level 3, for example, the objectives need to use words that support transfer, such as "demonstrate" or "implement" or "recommend" or "utilize." How these objectives are stated then determines the type of assessments and instructional strategies.

Instructional strategies should fulfill the learning objectives, provide for practice, and become a method for evaluation. You can assess the correctness of practice exercises as participants demonstrate knowledge and skills. You can monitor action plans, performance contracts, and learning contracts for use on the job. So, learning objectives becomes a linchpin between evaluation and design.

As you see, evaluation is not something you do at the end of delivery; rather it is a continuous, integrated process. Evaluation made part of the program development process can help programs succeed, as well as measure whether they do what they are intended to do. As you design the training course, get input from the client and representatives of the target audience at each stage in the design process. Not only does this help to ensure that the course is on target in regard to content, instructional strategies, and cultural fit, it also transfers ownership of the program from the designer to the client organization.

Think About This

For evaluation to be effective, several things must be present. First, evaluation must be linked to the business opportunity analysis, needs analysis, and learning objectives. Second, the feedback must be timely. The evaluation results must be provided to the appropriate people on a timely basis so decisions and changes can be made while the training program is still current. Third, evaluation must be conducted on an ongoing basis throughout the design process, and changes must be made immediately. Fourth, the training environment must support transfer. The effectiveness of an evaluation system is contingent upon an environment that supports transfer.

Demonstrating Value

When trainers think of adding value, they usually think about ROI. Yet, ROI requires transfer. If there is no transfer, there is no ROI for a training course. So, can you demonstrate value by demonstrating transfer? Most assuredly. Can you demonstrate transfer by others' testimonies? For example, a sales leadership program was offered to sales managers and directors. At each delivery, either a regional marketing vice president or an assistant vice president was present. After several deliveries, these individuals were making very positive comments about the course in their executive meetings. For them to do this, they had to see value.

The training organization cannot demonstrate value independent of the client organization. To be effective and demonstrate value, training must support the goals and strategies of the client's organization. Training must help the client achieve his or her objectives and fulfill strategies. As such, the training unit must build and maintain strong relationships with the clients, forging partnerships, allowing trainers to serve as internal consultants to line managers on performance and motivation issues, as well as training. If training is seen as a separate activity, not directly related to the operations of the organization, then it is difficult to demonstrate value. If, however, the training organization works in partnership with clients to achieve business results, then training is seen as a value-add partner.

To support the business outcomes of your clients, you must understand them and determine where you can add value. Each client objective must be analyzed and the training component identified. In addition, the training organization should develop positioning strategies to that frame the clients' view of the training organization. As the training organization partners with its clients and as the clients objectives are met, this partnership will allow the training function to gain credibility through demonstrated added value.

Basic Rule 22

The key to successful client partnerships is to gain access to your clients in multiple ways and to demonstrate competence, credibility, and the ability to help make them successful.

Becoming a partner is not easy but is necessary. Developing this partnership goes beyond delivering training courses and conducting evaluation. To better position yourself with your clients, you could

- offer to serve in a consulting capacity
- act as a coach to line management
- serve on work teams
- demonstrate the cost effectiveness of training programs
- perform as an advocate for change
- take actions to maintain high visibility of the HRD department.

Think About This

To successfully partner with clients, you must know and understand their business including their goals, strategies, customers, marketplace, products, and so forth. You also need to demonstrate business savvy. It is incumbent on the training organization to know and understand their clients' business and to communicate to them in language they understand. A good place to demonstrate this capability is in planning sessions with your clients. They are the clients; HRD is the provider. They have alternatives; you must partner and demonstrate value.

Readiness

In the Getting It Done section in chapter 1, you evaluated the readiness of your organization to go further in your evaluation efforts. That evaluation provided some direct, but narrow dimensions to start your thinking about evaluation and your organization. Yet, readiness involves more than just evaluation; it is also a culture issue.

The effectiveness of HRD programs is contingent on factors in the organization's corporate culture. Pit a good employee against a corporate culture that does not support HR programs, products, and services—and the corporate culture will win every time.

Employees who have been trained in a set of skills but work in a corporate culture that does not support those skills will eventually stop using them. Corporate culture governs whether learners utilize the skills they learned during training. The foundation for building a solid corporate culture supportive of training is the support of supervisors and senior management. Cultural factors include such things as

- *Climate:* Do the norms, values, and expectations of fellow employees and managers support the new behaviors that were just learned?
- *Time and timing:* Does the learner have the time to do things the way he or she was taught? Was there an opportunity to apply the new learning fairly immediately, or was there too great a delay?
- *Degree of fit:* Do organizational procedures, forms, and process agree with those taught during the training?
- *Supervisory support:* Does management budget for training? Are employees encouraged to attend training? Is there an expectation that employees will further develop their knowledge and skills? Is transfer supported?
- *Recognition and reward:* Are employees recognized for developing new skills? Is staff development a performance objective for managers? How is the acquisition of new knowledge, skills, and abilities recognized and rewarded at the unit, department, and organizational levels?

There are several methods that can be used to influence the culture to become supportive of training. First, hold managers accountable for the development of their people. Managers could have performance objectives related to people development.

Second, you could provide incentives for those using the newly acquired knowledge, skills, and abilities. The practices may vary from organization to organization, depending upon the work setting, subject matter, and other independent variables. In some instances, the incentive is merely the participants' desire to apply what they have learned and the intrinsic reward of seeing their goal achieved. In other cases, it may be necessary to tie the use of the training to either a formal appraisal process carried on by the organization or a similar method of evaluation by someone outside of the department. Giving challenging assignments with exposure to key individuals could serve as a good incentive benefiting both the individual and the organization.

Third, senior managers must not only communicate the importance of people development, but they must also model their support. They and their direct reports must engage in development and support it within the organization. They can also participate in the needs assessment or in training programs, become involved in follow-up action plans, commit resources to development, plan with participants the implementation of the learning prior to attendance, set the expectations that the new knowledge and skills will be used, and engage in follow-up coaching. Ceremonies are another good way to communicate culture. Executives could hand out the certificates at a closing ceremony or dinner; make it a graduation experience.

Fourth, senior management can provide the leadership role of a HRD advisory board to guide the development and implementation of the curriculum. They can help to establish a cross-function working committee for identification and use of internal resources for content, delivery, and evaluation.

Fifth, senior management should demand, and the training organization should initiate, the HRD organization's involvement in the strategic planning of the organization. HRD implications should be identified and strategies and goals established to help the organization be successful.

Next, management should recognize the new skills of participants through job assignments, peer teaching, and visible recognition in meetings and internal communications.

Last, the culture can be affected by communicating training successes. Stories can have a positive impact in changing or reinforcing culture. Some other ideas include the following:

▶ Institute weekly interdepartmental meetings to exchange information and ideas on projects, training issues, and to receive input from workers in other areas.
▶ Devise a simple form for reporting lessons learned and base future training program examples on these real scenarios.
▶ Create an employee-of-the-month program based on the use of trained skills, knowledge, behaviors, and abilities. Publicize the name of the honored employee and explain why that person was selected.

Symbols can also be used to convey meaning. Many organizations use certificates, T-shirts, mugs, portfolios, and the like as ways to convey meaning. Wooden plaques with the president's signature signal a message of support. Book give-a-ways can carry the training beyond the classroom or learning experience. One organization created a special edition of *The Classic Touch: Lessons in Leadership from Homer to Hemingway* by J. Clemens and D. Mayer (McGraw-Hill, 1999) to support its leadership development efforts. Another organization had as part of its strategic program a competitive war game. The winning team members received camouflage hats embroidered with the message "We Won the Business." Those hats became sought-after symbols of success.

Getting It Done

Developing readiness and a culture supportive of training is not easy. It can be done, however. Start where readiness exists. Nurture, recognize, and support the areas that are already supporting training efforts. Develop key relationships and demonstrate value. Show your clients how you can be a valued strategic partner as they strive to meet their business objectives. Exercise 9-1 can help you think about becoming a strategic partner.

Exercise 9-1. Demonstrating your value.

In the space below, for one client or a business unit objective that has a training requirement, write the objective, the client's strategies to achieve that objective, and the initial training requirement. Then indicate how you—the HRD professional—can demonstrate value.

Objective:

_____

_____

_____

Strategies to Accomplish the Objective:

1. _____

_____

2. _____

_____

3. _____

_____

(continued on page 170)

Exercise 9-1. Demonstrating your value (continued).

4. _____

_____

Training Requirement:

_____

_____

_____

_____

_____

Value Demonstration:

_____

_____

_____

_____

_____

As organizations continue to strive for competitive advantage, human capital is the key to that advantage. Developing and maximizing human capital for individual and business unit success is your business. The time is now, so seize the moment! Good luck with all your evaluation efforts!

Appendix A
Rating Guides for Courseware and Facilitation

■ ■

The four levels of evaluation assess a course delivery from the standpoints of reaction, learning, transfer, and impact or results. They do not assess the overall course delivery or the quality of facilitation. Rating guides for delivery and facilitation take a much broader view by assessing the entirety of a course and the facilitation.

Rating guides for delivery are generally scaled 0–5, with a score of 0 meaning missing/absent and 5 meaning high/excellent. Rating guides for facilitator assessment are usually scaled from 0–4, with 0 being "not at all" and 4 being "to a very great extent."

Figure A-1 is a rating guide for *classroom delivery*. Such instruments review the quality and completeness of the facilitator guide, design issues, the evaluation plan, learning strategies, participants' guides, media, and the train-the-trainer process.

Figure A-2 is a rating guide for *online delivery*. This instrument reviews the quality and completeness of the more general aspects of the course, design, evaluation plan, learning strategies, technical support, and any enhanced capabilities.

Figure A-3 is a rating guide for a *self-study*. It covers the quality and completeness from a general aspect and then addresses design issues, learning strategies, and the evaluation plan.

Figure A-4 is a rating guide for *facilitation*. It is a weighted instrument that allows you to distribute 100 points across the six major areas of assessment. Then, the evaluator rates the facilitator according to the areas of assessment. By multiplying the weight by the rating and summing the data, you arrive at a score between 0 and 400. Your HRD organization then sets the criterion score for acceptable performance.

For assistance in using these instruments, you may contact the author at donpag@bellsouth.net.

Figure A-1. Rating guide for HRD review—classroom delivery.

A six-point rating scale (0–5) is used for the HRD quality review:

5 **High/Excellent:** Evidence of quality exists, and the material is of excellent and highly consistent quality. The training material and/or learning experience may be very effective due to the excellent or outstanding qualities of the course.

4 **Better than level 3 but not at level 5**

3 **Good/Consistent:** Evidence of high quality exists, and the material is of good or consistent quality. The training material and/or learning experience may be effective due to the presence of this factor or quality of the course.

2 **Better than level 1 but not at level 3**

1 **Poor/Inconsistent:** Little evidence of quality exists; the quality is poor or inconsistent. The training material and/or learning experience may be less effective if quality is not improved or consistently applied.

0 **Missing/Absent:** No evidence exists. The training material and/or learning experience are incomplete without this factor or quality being present.

Facilitator Guide	The quality of this course is:						Comments
	0 Absent/ Missing	**1** Poor/ Inconsistent	**2** ...	**3** Good/ Consistent	**4** ...	**5** High/ Excellent	
1. Course material is well organized according to a logical flow or sequence.	0	1	2	3	4	5	
2. Timelines are provided for each module.	0	1	2	3	4	5	
3. There is a link to the participant guide/materials and media.	0	1	2	3	4	5	
4. Course content links to and supports learning objectives.	0	1	2	3	4	5	
5. There is a course roadmap or overall program plan.	0	1	2	3	4	5	
6. There is a listing of all support materials, media, supplies, and so forth.	0	1	2	3	4	5	

Design Issues	The quality of this course is:						Comments
	0 Absent/ Missing	**1** Poor/ Inconsistent	**2** …	**3** Good/ Consistent	**4** …	**5** High/ Excellent	
1. There are course goals indicating overall purpose.	0	1	2	3	4	5	
2. There are established learning objectives.	0	1	2	3	4	5	
• They are measurable.	0	1	2	3	4	5	
• They are written for level 2 (learning) and 3 (transfer to the job).	0	1	2	3	4	5	
3. There is a logical sequence for each module (introduction or warm-up, presentation of content, practice, application, summary).	0	1	2	3	4	5	

Evaluation Plan	**0**	**1**	**2**	**3**	**4**	**5**	
1. The evaluation plan is comprehensive to level 2.	0	1	2	3	4	5	
2. Instruments for evaluation levels 1 and 2 have been developed.	0	1	2	3	4	5	
3. Instruments for evaluation level 2 provide for knowledge assessment (pretest, posttest, in-class).	0	1	2	3	4	5	
4. Instruments for evaluation level 2 provide for practice/application assessment.	0	1	2	3	4	5	
5. Level 2 and 3 instruments align with the learning objectives.	0	1	2	3	4	5	

(continued on page 174)

Figure A-1. Rating guide for HRD review—classroom delivery (continued).

Instructional/Learning Strategies	The quality of this course is:						Comments
	0 Absent/ Missing	**1** Poor/ Inconsistent	**2** ...	**3** Good/ Consistent	**4** ...	**5** High/ Excellent	
1. There are opportunities to apply course content to the job (practice exercises, action plan, case study, and so forth).	0	1	2	3	4	5	
2. There are complete instructions with each instructional/learning strategy.	0	1	2	3	4	5	
3. The instructional strategies support the content and learning objectives.	0	1	2	3	4	5	
4. Skill practice exercises reinforce course content.	0	1	2	3	4	5	
5. Instructional strategies allow for practice and application.	0	1	2	3	4	5	
6. There are varied types of instructional strategies (small group work, case study, role play, facilitated discussion, demonstration, peer teaching, and so forth).	0	1	2	3	4	5	
7. The activities have complete debrief to support learning points.	0	1	2	3	4	5	
8. The appropriate instructional strategies were used to support learning. • Lecture: to deliver key information when learners are not familiar with the content • Facilitation/group discussion: to deliver information and content when learners are familiar with the subject • Modeling/demonstration: to help learners acquire a skill or behavior • Case study: to help learners analyze problems and provide solution • Role play: to train for interpersonal skills	0	1	2	3	4	5	
9. There are instruments for transfer, such as a performance contract, action planning, or learning contract.	0	1	2	3	4	5	

The quality of this course is:

	0 Absent/ Missing	1 Poor/ Inconsistent	2	3 Good/ Consistent	4	5 High/ Excellent	Comments
Participant Guide and Materials							
1. The participant manual allows for interaction and learning, that is, engages the participant.	0	1	2	3	4	5	
2. Pre-course reading materials support the learning.	0	1	2	3	4	5	
3. Text is easy to read.	0	1	2	3	4	5	
4. There is an easy transition between the participant guide and other materials.	0	1	2	3	4	5	
Media							
1. There is a mix of media or visual aids (overheads, video, flipcharts, whiteboards, wallboards, and so forth).	0	1	2	3	4	5	
2. Overhead media follow high-quality media standards. • 6 x 6 or 8 x 8 format (that is, six words per line, six lines per overhead or PowerPoint slide) • At least 18-point font for small groups; 24 point for larger groups with titles 30 point • No red or yellow font colors	0	1	2	3	4	5	

(continued on page 176)

Figure A-1. Rating guide for HRD review—classroom delivery (continued).

Train-the-Trainer Process	The quality of this course is:					Comments
	0 Absent/ Missing	1 Poor/ Inconsistent	2 …	3 Good/ Consistent	4 …	5 High/ Excellent	
1. There are documented criteria to select qualified instructors/facilitators, including: • knowledgeable of the call center industry • years of experience in a call center industry recognition • knowledge of the subject matter • years of experience as a facilitator • educational level • credibility with the target audience • professional image (dress, vocabulary)	0	1	2	3	4	5	
2. There is a documented train-the-trainer process: • Selection of facilitators is based on a facilitation selection process. • Selected facilitators are involved in the design/development process. • Selected facilitators attend pilot. • Train-the-trainer session is conducted for each course to train the facilitators on the content, learning strategies, and assessments. • Selected facilitators co-teach the course with a trained individual. • Selected facilitators deliver the course with a trained facilitator observing and providing feedback.	0	1	2	3	4	5	

Reprinted with permission from Performance Advantage Group, 2004.

Figure A-2. Rating guide for HRD review—online.

A six-point rating scale (0–5) is used for the HRD quality review:

5 **High/Excellent:** Evidence of quality exists, and the material is of excellent and highly consistent quality. The training material and/or learning experience may be very effective due to the excellent or outstanding qualities of the course.

4 **Better than level 3 but not at level 5**

3 **Good/Consistent:** Evidence of high quality exists, and the material is of good or consistent quality. The training material and/or learning experience may be effective due to the presence of this factor or quality in the course.

2 **Better than level 1 but not at level 3**

1 **Poor/Inconsistent:** Little evidence of quality exists; the quality is poor or inconsistent. The training material and/or learning experience may be less effective if quality is not improved or consistently applied.

0 **Missing/Absent:** No evidence exists. The training material and/or learning experience are incomplete without this factor or quality being present.

General/Overview	The quality of this course is:						Comments
	0 Absent/ Missing	**1** Poor/ Inconsistent	**2** …	**3** Good/ Consistent	**4** …	**5** High/ Excellent	
1. There is an introduction section that outlines the purpose of the course and provides instructions. • There is a "navigational tour" to describe the navigation buttons of the interface.	0	1	2	3	4	5	
2. Text is easy to read.	0	1	2	3	4	5	
3. There is just-in-time access to content.	0	1	2	3	4	5	
4. Course allows learners to determine their own module(s) or learning path.	0	1	2	3	4	5	

(continued on page 178)

Figure A-2. Rating guide for HRD review—online (continued).

The quality of this course is:

General/Overview (continued)	0 Absent/ Missing	1 Poor/ Inconsistent	2	3 Good/ Consistent	4	5 High/ Excellent	Comments
5. There is ease of navigation (how learners move through the course):							
• A course map is provided.							
• Colors, graphics, or symbols help users identify where they are in the course.	0	1	2	3	4	5	
• There are exit options that allow learners to return to specific places in the course.							

Design	0	1	2	3	4	5	
1. The course has stated goal(s) indicating overall purpose.	0	1	2	3	4	5	
2. There are established learning objectives:	0	1	2	3	4	5	
• They are measurable.	0	1	2	3	4	5	
• They are written for level 2 (learning).	0	1	2	3	4	5	
• They are written for level 3 (transfer/application)	0	1	2	3	4	5	
3. The course content links to and supports learning objectives.	0	1	2	3	4	5	
4. There is a consistent sequence or format for each module (introduction, content, practice, application, summary).	0	1	2	3	4	5	
5. There is consistency of style throughout the course (fonts, colors, use of graphics, photos, and so forth).	0	1	2	3	4	5	
6. There is a logical learning path.	0	1	2	3	4	5	
7. There is a modular approach allowing for short blocks of study.	0	1	2	3	4	5	
8. There are motivational components to keep learners engaged (testing, game, novelty, humor, surprise).	0	1	2	3	4	5	

Design (continued)		The quality of this course is:						Comments
		0 Absent/ Missing	**1** Poor/ Inconsistent	**2** ...	**3** Good/ Consistent	**4** ...	**5** High/ Excellent	
9. The course's technical design promotes a smooth flow of learning: • Screens only refresh changed information. • There are no delays or excessive levels to navigate. • All non-text information (graphics, audio, video, animation) is easy to view/hear and does not cause delays.		0	1	2	3	4	5	
10. There is a variety of media to present concepts.		0	1	2	3	4	5	
11. There is quality of text, graphics, and/or animation: • The graphics support learning to illustrate concepts, shape interactive practices, or challenge learners. • The graphics and/or animations enhance the learning process within practice, test, examples, and text.		0	1	2	3	4	5	

Evaluation Plan		0	1	2	3	4	5	
1. There is a level 1 evaluation for feedback.		0	1	2	3	4	5	
2. There are instruments for level 2 (pretest, posttest, interim); pre-assessments and testing out of content.		0	1	2	3	4	5	
3. Level 2 instruments align with the learning objectives.		0	1	2	3	4	5	
4. Online practice assessments require mastery before course completion: • Assessment feedback/scoring is provided.		0	1	2	3	4	5	

(continued on page 180)

Figure A-2. Rating guide for HRD review—online (continued).

	The quality of this course is:					Comments
Instructional/Learning Strategies	**0** Absent/ Missing	**1** Poor/ Inconsistent	**2** ...	**3** Good/ Consistent	**4** ...	**5** High/ Excellent	
1. Practice activities/exercises reinforce course content and learning objectives.	0	1	2	3	4	5	
2. There are complete instructions with each of the learning activities/exercises.	0	1	2	3	4	5	
3. The learning activities/exercises have complete and correct answers.	0	1	2	3	4	5	
4. Instructional strategies, tools, and instruments provide for the application of knowledge to the job.	0	1	2	3	4	5	
5. There are printable job aids.	0	1	2	3	4	5	
6. There are a variety of activity and scenario settings (inbound, outbound, service, sales, account closing, general inquiry, and so forth).	0	1	2	3	4	5	
7. Knowledge/skill gap analysis is used as a pre-assessment tool to allow learners to move past certain content if they succeed in that area of the pre-assessment.	0	1	2	3	4	5	

Technical Support	**0**	**1**	**2**	**3**	**4**	**5**	
1. There is administrative support available.	0	1	2	3	4	5	
2. There is technical support available.	0	1	2	3	4	5	
3. Quality of service (QOS) statement indicates: • What will be provided • How it will be provided • Level of system/network reliability (99.999% is ideal.)	0	1	2	3	4	5	

Enhanced Capabilities	The quality of this course is:						Comments
	0 Absent/ Missing	**1** Poor/ Inconsistent	**2** ...	**3** Good/ Consistent	**4** ...	**5** High/ Excellent	
1. The course contains streaming audio (voice and/or sound effects) and video that enhances learning. • It is integrated into the instructional design.	0	1	2	3	4	5	
2. There is collaboration among learners that enhances learning: • It is integrated into the instructional design.	0	1	2	3	4	5	
3. There is online mentoring (virtual or person) that enhances learning: • It is integrated into the instructional design. • Mentor and learner have required outcomes.	0	1	2	3	4	5	
4. Online interactions link to and support learning objectives.	0	1	2	3	4	5	

Reprinted with permission from Performance Advantage Group, 2004.

Figure A-3. Rating guide for HRD review—self-studies.

A six-point rating scale (0–5) is used for the HRD quality review:

5 **High/Excellent:** Evidence of quality exists, and the material is of excellent and highly consistent quality. The training material and/or learning experience may be very effective due to the excellent or outstanding qualities of the course.

4 **Better than level 3 but not at level 5**

3 **Good/Consistent:** Evidence of high quality exists, and the material is of good or consistent quality. The training material and/or learning experience may be effective due to the presence of this factor or quality in the course.

2 **Better than level 1 but not at level 3**

1 **Poor/Inconsistent:** Little evidence of quality exists; the quality is poor or inconsistent. The training material and/or learning experience may be less effective if quality is not improved or consistently applied.

0 **Missing/Absent:** No evidence exists. The training material and/or learning experience are incomplete without this factor or quality being present.

General/Overview	The quality of this course is:						Comments
	0 Absent/ Missing	**1** Poor/ Inconsistent	**2** …	**3** Good/ Consistent	**4** …	**5** High/ Excellent	
1. There is a table of contents.	0	1	2	3	4	5	
2. There is a bibliography or listing of references.	0	1	2	3	4	5	
3. There is an introduction section telling the purpose of the self-study and how to use it.	0	1	2	3	4	5	
4. Text is easy to read, incorporating graphics and white space.	0	1	2	3	4	5	
5. The material allows for interaction and facilitates learning; it engages the participant.	0	1	2	3	4	5	

The quality of this course is:

Design Issues	0 Absent/ Missing	1 Poor/ Inconsistent	2	3 Good/ Consistent	4	5 High/ Excellent	Comments
1. Course has stated goal(s) indicating overall purpose.	0	1	2	3	4	5	
2. There are established learning objectives:	0	1	2	3	4	5	
• They are measurable.	0	1	2	3	4	5	
• They are written for level 2 (learning and application).	0	1	2	3	4	5	
• They are written for level 3 (transfer to the job).	0	1	2	3	4	5	
3. Course content links to and supports learning objectives.	0	1	2	3	4	5	
4. There is a consistent sequence, format, or flow for each module.	0	1	2	3	4	5	

Instructional/Learning Strategies	0	1	2	3	4	5	
1. Practice activities/exercises reinforce course content.	0	1	2	3	4	5	
2. There are complete instructions with each of the activities/exercises.	0	1	2	3	4	5	
3. The activities/exercises have complete answers.	0	1	2	3	4	5	
4. The activities/exercises support the content and learning objectives.	0	1	2	3	4	5	
5. There are strategies/tools/instruments for application to the job.	0	1	2	3	4	5	
6. There are motivational components to keep learners engaged (testing, exercises, application, and so forth).	0	1	2	3	4	5	

(continued on page 184)

Figure A-3. Rating guide for HRD review—self-studies (continued).

Evaluation Plan	The quality of this course is:						Comments
	0 Absent/ Missing	**1** Poor/ Inconsistent	**2** ...	**3** Good/ Consistent	**4** ...	**5** High/ Excellent	
1. There is a level 1 (reaction) evaluation for feedback.	0	1	2	3	4	5	
2. There are instruments for level 2 (learning and application) (pretest, posttest, interim test, and so forth).	0	1	2	3	4	5	
3. Level 2 instruments align with the learning objectives.	0	1	2	3	4	5	

Reprinted with permission from Performance Advantage Group, 2004.

Figure A-4. Rating guide for facilitation.

Below is a list of behaviors describing the demonstration of facilitation/presentation skills. As an assessor, weight each behavior with the total being 100. Then use the following scale to indicate the extent to which the individual demonstrates the listed behaviors.

0 = not at all   1 = to very little extent   2 = to a moderate extent   3 = to a great extent   4 = to a very great extent

	Weight	0	1	2	3	4	TOTAL
Credibility							
1. Demonstrates appropriate personal and professional behavior							
2. Demonstrates subject content knowledge (depth and breadth)							
3. Makes linkages to organizational realities							
Learning Environment							
4. Involves participants in establishing and maintaining the learning environment							
5. Uses opening (warm-up) activities to gain participant involvement							
6. Manages group interaction, draws in quiet participants, and manages participants who try to monopolize the interaction							
7. Integrates adult learning principles into the course delivery							
Communication Skills							
8. Uses appropriate verbal and nonverbal communication methodology							
9. Uses examples that are familiar to the participants							
10. Provides complete and timely feedback to participants							
11. Provides time for participants to structure/frame and ask questions and/or voice concerns/issues							
Presentation/Facilitation Skills							
12. Effectively uses voice (tone, projection, inflection), gestures, and eye contact							
13. Effectively uses examples, personal experiences, stories, and humor							
14. Effectively uses various questioning techniques							
15. Effectively paraphrases/restates participants' questions, comments, and observations							
16. Promotes participant discussion and involvement							
17. Keeps discussion on topic and activities focused on outcomes							

(continued on page 186)

Figure A-4. Rating guide for facilitation (continued).

	Weight	0	1	2	3	4	TOTAL
Instructional/Learning Strategies							
18. Implements a variety of instructional/learning strategies (such as guided discussions, case studies, role plays, small group work with feedback, assessments)							
19. Plans and facilitates debriefs so all learning is processed							
20. Adjusts activities, time, pace, content, and sequencing to accommodate specific learner needs							
Media							
21. Uses media (video, overheads, computer projection, wallboards, props, flipcharts) effectively							
22. Demonstrates ability to substitute, change, or add media as needed							
TOTAL	100						

Upon completion, multiply the weight of each behavior by the rating and add up the total column. The total will be between 0 and 400. This is the participant's assessment score. The criterion reference score for passing is _____.

References

Barksdale, S., and T. Lund. (2001). *Rapid Evaluation.* Alexandria, VA: ASTD.

Bloom, B.S. (editor). (1956). *Taxonomy of Educational Objectives: The Classification of Educational Goals: Handbook I, Cognitive Domain.* New York: Longmans, Green.

Broad, M., and J. Newstrom. (1992). *Transfer of Training.* Reading, MA: Addison-Wesley.

Eyler, Janet. (No year). "The PILL Model of Evaluation." Nashville: Vanderbilt University.

Kirkpatrick, D.L. (1994). *Evaluating Training Programs: The Four Levels.* San Francisco: Berrett-Koehler Publishers.

Lewin, K. (1975). *Field Theory in Social Science.* Westport, CT: Greenwood.

Makridakis, S. (1989). *Forecasting Methods for Management,* 5th edition. New York: Wiley.

Phillips, J. (1994). *In Action: Measuring Return on Investment.* Alexandria, VA: ASTD.

Phillips, J. (1997). *Handbook of Training Evaluation and Measurement Methods,* 3rd edition. Houston: Gulf Publishing Company.

Additional Resources

Adult Learning

Knowles, M., E.F. Holton, and R.A. Swanson. (1998). *The Adult Learner: The Definitive Classic in Adult Education and Human Resource Development,* 5th edition. Houston: Gulf Publishing.

Merriam, S.B. (editor). (2001). *New Directions for Adult and Continuing Education.* San Francisco: Jossey-Bass.

Merriam, S.B., and R.S. Cafarella. (1998). *Learning in Adulthood: A Comprehensive Guide.* San Francisco: Jossey-Bass.

Vella, J. (2002). *Learning to Listen, Learning to Teach: The Power of Dialogue in Educating Adults.* San Francisco: Jossey-Bass.

Facilitator Competencies and Facilitation Skills

Eitington, J.E. (2002). *The Winning Trainer: Winning Ways to Involve People in Learning,* 4th edition. Woburn, MA: Butterworth-Heinemann.

Hunter, D., A. Bailey, and B. Taylor. (1995). *The Art of Facilitation.* Tucson: Fisher Books.

Justice, T., and D.W. Jamieson. (1999). *The Facilitator's Fieldbook.* New York: AMA-COM.

Kearney, L. (1995). *The Facilitator's Toolkit.* Amherst, MA: HRD Press.

Kinlaw, D. (1996). *The ASTD Trainer's Sourcebook: Facilitation Skills.* New York: McGraw-Hill.

Leatherman, D. (1990). *The Training Trilogy: Facilitation Skills.* Amherst, MA: HRD Press.

McCain, D., and D. Tobey. (2004). *Facilitation Basics.* Alexandria, VA: ASTD.

Rumsey, T.A. (1996). *Not Just Games: Strategic Uses of Experiential Learning to Drive Business Results.* Dubuque, IA: Kendall-Hunt.

Shapiro, L.T. (1995). *Training Effectiveness Handbook.* New York: McGraw-Hill.

Wheeling, S.A. (1990). *Facilitating Training Groups.* New York: Praeger.

General HRD Material

Charney, C., and K. Conway. (1998). *The Trainer's Tool Kit.* New York: AMACOM.

Craig, R. (1987). *Training and Development Handbook,* 3rd edition. New York: McGraw-Hill.

Mitchell, G. (1992). *The Trainer's Handbook: The AMA Guide to Effective Training.* Belmont, CA: Lake Publishing.

Rosenbaum, S., and J. Williams. (2004). *Learning Paths.* San Diego: Pfeiffer.

Instructional Development and Learning Activity Development

Anglin, G. (1991). *Instructional Technology: Past, Present and Future.* Englewood, CO: Libraries Unlimited.

Barca, M., and K. Cobb. (1994). *Beginnings & Endings: Creative Warm-Ups & Closure Activities.* Amherst, MA: HRD Press.

Clark, R. (1989). *Developing Technical Training: A Structured Approach for the Development of Classroom and Computer-Based Instructional Materials.* Reading, MA: Addison-Wesley.

Hattori, R.A., and J. Wycoff. (2004). *Innovation Training.* Alexandria, VA: ASTD.

Hodell, C. (2000). *ISD From the Ground Up: A No-Nonsense Approach to Instructional Design.* Alexandria, VA: ASTD.

Jones, K. (1997). *Creative Events for Trainers.* New York: McGraw-Hill.

Leatherman, D. (1990). *The Training Trilogy: Designing Programs.* Amherst, MA: HRD Press.

McCain, D. (1999). *Creating Training Courses When You're Not a Trainer.* Alexandria, VA: ASTD.

Nadler, L. (1989). *Designing Training Programs: The Critical Events Model.* New York: Addison-Wesley.

Newstrom, J.W., and E.E. Scannell. (1980). *Games Trainers Play.* New York: McGraw-Hill.

Newstrom, J.W., and E.E. Scannell. (1983). *More Games Trainers Play.* New York: McGraw-Hill.

Newstrom, J.W., and E.E. Scannell. (1991). *Still More Games Trainers Play.* New York: McGraw-Hill.

Newstrom, J.W., and E.E. Scannell. (1994). *Even More Games Trainers Play.* New York: McGraw-Hill.

Silberman, M., and K. Lawson. (1995). *101 Ways to Make Training Active.* San Diego: Pfeiffer.

Silberman, M. (1990). *Active Training: Handbook of Techniques, Designs, Case Examples, and Tips.* New York: Lexington Books.

Measurement and Evaluation

Barksdale, S., and T. Lund. (2001). *Rapid Evaluation.* Alexandria, VA: ASTD.

Bartrow, S., and B. Gibson. (1999). *Evaluating Training.* Amherst, MA: HRD Press.

Bassie, L. (2004). *What Works: Assessment, Development, and Measurement.* Alexandria, VA: ASTD.

Brinkerhoff, R.O. (1987). *Achieving Results From Training.* San Francisco: Jossey-Bass.

Combs, W.L., and S.V. Falletta. (2004). *The Targeted Evaluation Process.* Alexandria, VA: ASTD.

Dixon, N. (1990). *Evaluation: A Tool for Improving Quality.* San Diego: University Associates.

Hodges, T.K. (2002). *Linking Learning and Performance: A Practical Guide to Measuring Learning and On-the-Job Application.* Woburn, MA: Butterworth-Heinemann.

Horton, W. (2004). *Evaluating E-Learning.* Alexandria, VA: ASTD.

Parry, S. (2004). *Evaluating the Impact of Training.* Alexandria, VA: ASTD.

Phillips, J., and M. Broad. (1997). *In Action: Transferring Learning to the Workplace.* Alexandria, VA: ASTD.

Phillips, J., P.P. Phillips, and T.K. Hodges. (2004). *Make Training Evaluation Work.* Alexandria, VA: ASTD.

Russ-Eft, D., and H. Preskill. (2001). *Evaluation in Organizations.* Cambridge, MA: Perseus Publishing.

Spencer, L. (1986). *Calculating Human Resource Costs and Benefits.* New York: John Wiley & Sons.

Stadius, R. (editor). (1999). *More Evaluation Instruments: ASTD Trainer's Toolkit.* Alexandria, VA: ASTD.

Swanson, R., and E. Holton. (1999). *Results? How to Assess Performance, Learning, and Perceptions in Organizations.* San Francisco: Berrett-Koehler.

Needs Analysis

Gupta, K. (1999). *A Practical Guide to Needs Assessment.* San Francisco: Jossey-Bass/Pfeiffer.

Leatherman, D. (1990). *The Training Trilogy: Assessing Needs.* Amherst, MA: HRD Press.

Mager, R.F., and P. Pipe. (1989). *Analyzing Performance Problems.* Belmont, CA: Pittman Learning.

Phillips, J., and E.F. Holton, III. (1995). *In Action: Conducting Needs Assessment.* Alexandria, VA: ASTD.

Robinson, D.G., and J.C. Robinson. (1989). *Training for Impact: How to Link Training to Business Needs and Measure the Results.* San Francisco: Jossey-Bass.

Rossett, A. (1987). *Training Needs Assessment.* New York: Educational Technology Publishers.

Swanson, R. (1996). *Analysis for Improving Performance.* San Francisco: Berrett-Koehler.

Zemke, R., and T. Kramlinger. (1982). *Figuring Things Out: A Trainer's Guide to Needs & Task Analysis.* Reading, MA: Addison-Wesley.

Presentation Skills

Becker, D., and P.B. Becker. (1994). *Powerful Presentation Skills.* Chicago: Irwin Professional Publishing.

Burn, B.E. (1996). *Flip Chart Power: Secrets of the Masters.* San Diego: Pfeiffer.

Jolles, R.L. (2000). *How to Run Seminars and Workshops: Presentation Skills for Consultants, Trainers, and Teachers.* New York: John Wiley & Sons.

Peoples, D.A. (1997). *Presentations Plus: David Peoples' Proven Techniques,* revised edition. New York: John Wiley & Sons.

Pike, R., and D. Arch. (1997). *Dealing With Difficult Participants: 127 Practical Strategies for Minimizing Resistance and Maximizing Results in Your Presentations.* San Francisco: Jossey-Bass.

Rosania, R. (2003). *Presentation Basics.* Alexandria, VA: ASTD.

Silberman, M., and K. Clark. (1999). *101 Ways to Make Meetings Active: Surefire Ideas to Engage Your Group.* San Francisco: Pfeiffer.

Stettner, M. (2002). *Mastering Business Presentations.* McLean, VA: The National Institute of Business Management.

Zelazny, G. (1999). *Say It With Presentations: How to Design and Deliver Successful Business Presentations.* New York: McGraw-Hill Trade.

Strategic HRD

Gilley, J., and A. Maycunich. (1998). *Strategically Integrated HRD: Partnering to Maximize Organizational Performance.* Reading, MA: Addison-Wesley.

Gomez-Mejia, L., D. Balkin, and R. Cardy. (2004). *Managing Human Resources,* 4th edition. Upper Saddle River, NJ: Prentice Hall.

Hudson, W. (1993). *Intellectual Capital: How to Build It, Enhance It, Use It.* New York: John Wiley & Sons.

Mathis, R., and J. Jackson. (2003). *Human Resource Management,* 10th edition. Mason, OH: South-Western.

Phillips, J. (1996). *Accountability in Human Resource Management.* Houston: Gulf Publishing Company.

Sevenson, R., and M. Rinderer. (1992). *The Training and Development Strategic Plan Workbook.* Englewood Cliffs, NJ: Prentice Hall.

Walton, J. (1999). *Strategic Human Resource Development.* London: Guildhall University/Financial Times Management/Prentice Hall.

About the Author

Donald V. McCain is founder and principal of Performance Advantage Group, an organization dedicated to helping companies gain competitive advantage through the development of their human resources. With more than 28 years of corporate and consulting experience, McCain's focus is on design and development of custom learning experiences in leadership, sales and marketing, call center management, and many areas of professional development that result in improved business unit and individual performance.

He also consults in HRD processes, including design/development, competency identification and development, certification, evaluation (including transfer and ROI), presentation and facilitation, and managing and marketing the HRD function. Most of his clients are *Fortune* 100 companies across various industries. His work is international in scope. McCain has also consulted with many new consultants on the business side of training consulting.

McCain has a bachelor's degree in business administration, a master's degree of divinity, a master's degree of business administration with a concentration in HR and marketing, as well as a doctorate in education in HRD from Vanderbilt University. He is a member of ASTD and the American Management Association International (AMAI), and a former member of the Academy of Human Resource Development (AHRD). In addition, McCain is currently a visiting professor at the school of business at Tennessee State University and a former adjunct professor for the school of management at Belmont University. McCain also teaches for the University of Phoenix. He served previously as an adjunct assistant professor of leadership and organizations for Vanderbilt University.

He is author of the book *Creating Training Courses (When You're Not a Trainer)* (ASTD, 1999) and co-author of *Facilitation Basics* with Deb Tobey (ASTD, 2004). He also wrote the lead article for *HRfocus,* "Aligning Training With Business Objectives" (February, 1999). Additionally, he has published several evaluation instruments.

McCain lives in Nashville, Tennessee, with his wife, Kathy, and their two boys, Weston and Colin. He also has two married daughters, Kimberly and Karla. Donald McCain may be contacted at donpag@bellsouth.net.